Romeo and Juliet

William Shakespeare

Guide written by John Mahoney

Coventry C

A *Letts* **Literature Guide for GCSE**

Contents

Who's who in *Romeo and Juliet*

Romeo

He that hath steerage of my course, Direct my sail

At the beginning of the play Romeo is an <u>immature</u> and <u>impulsive</u> boy who imagines that he is in love with Rosaline. His talk is full of bookish and <u>artificial expressions</u> of emotion and he seems to be wallowing in <u>self-pity</u>. When he meets Juliet and falls in love with her, this has a <u>dramatic</u> <u>effect</u> on his character. He becomes more <u>mature</u> and even attempts to make peace with Tybalt, Juliet's argumentative and aggressive cousin. Despite his new-found maturity and tolerance of the Capulets, Romeo remains impetuous. He has <u>one</u> <u>fixed</u> <u>idea</u> (marriage to Juliet) and, within that, simply <u>reacts</u> <u>to circumstances</u>. He responds to plans thought up by others (Friar Lawrence, Juliet or the Nurse) and his <u>mood</u> <u>swings</u> from despair to joy, even within one scene, for example, Act 3 Sc 3.

Juliet

My only love sprung from my only hate

As with Romeo, once they have met, there is only one point of focus in Juliet's life. However, she is presented rather differently from Romeo as we see her in a much more <u>convincing</u> <u>family</u> <u>situation</u>, where the coldness of her mother suggests why Juliet forms her opinions for herself. Despite her age, not quite fourteen, Juliet shows remarkable <u>independence</u> <u>and</u> <u>maturity</u>, but she is <u>obedient</u> to her parents until her love for Romeo makes such obedience impossible. She is <u>intelligent</u> <u>and</u> <u>perceptive</u>, possibly more so than Romeo. She is <u>utterly</u> <u>loyal</u> to Romeo and defies the whole world for him. She is prepared to risk taking a dangerous drug to fake death so that she can escape to be with him. She <u>accepts</u> <u>death</u> <u>willingly</u> at the end of the play, when fate has destroyed their lives.

Nurse

> *I think it best you married with the county . . .*
> *Romeo's a dishclout to him*

The Nurse's position in the Capulet household is <u>superior</u> to that of a normal servant. Juliet seems to have <u>taken</u> <u>the</u> <u>place</u> of the daughter she once had, and everything she does, she does for Juliet's benefit. She is a <u>simple</u> <u>soul</u> who is an easy target for Mercutio's lewd ribbing. She is <u>long-winded</u> as well as rather <u>rude</u> <u>and</u> <u>bawdy</u>, but she seems <u>sincere</u> and makes the audience laugh with her rather than at her. The Nurse is Juliet's <u>confidante</u> <u>and</u> <u>helper</u> for much of the play, but <u>forfeits</u> <u>her</u> <u>trust</u> when she advises marriage to Paris after Romeo's banishment. Juliet is shocked both by her <u>disloyalty</u> to Romeo and her lack of moral sense in advocating a <u>bigamous</u> <u>marriage</u>.

Friar Lawrence

> **66** *And here I stand both to impeach and purge* **99**

Friar Lawrence is a <u>respectable</u> <u>and</u> <u>well-meaning</u> ally of Romeo and Juliet. It is his plan which goes wrong and causes the final tragedy. He is a <u>kindly</u> but rather <u>unworldly</u> man, who thinks himself careful and wise but who proves to be over-ambitious in his plans. His <u>intentions</u> <u>seem</u> <u>good</u>, but he is <u>too</u> <u>optimistic</u> in hoping that the marriage of Romeo and Juliet will bring the two feuding families together. In the end it is their deaths which bring the Montagues and Capulets to their senses. At the end the Friar is revealed as a timid man when he <u>runs</u> <u>away</u>, leaving Juliet alone in the tomb.

Mercutio

> **66** *If love be rough with you, be rough with love* **99**

Mercutio bursts onto the scene with his <u>lively</u> <u>and</u> <u>bawdy</u> <u>wit</u>. His <u>brilliantly</u> <u>imaginative</u> <u>language</u> contrasts sharply with that of his melancholy friend Romeo and the sensible Benvolio. Mercutio lives life to the full: he is <u>witty</u>, <u>eloquent</u>, <u>loves</u> <u>to</u> <u>hear</u> <u>himself</u> <u>talk</u> and <u>does</u> <u>not</u> <u>suffer</u> <u>fools</u> <u>gladly</u>. He seems to take neither <u>life</u> <u>nor</u> <u>death</u> <u>very</u> <u>seriously</u>. He is one of Shakespeare's most bawdy characters and his language <u>contrasts</u> with that of the maturing Romeo. His <u>profane</u> <u>view</u> <u>of</u> <u>love</u> emphasises the strength and purity of Romeo's mature love for Juliet. Mercutio is <u>intensely</u> <u>loyal</u> to Romeo and intervenes on his behalf against Tybalt with fatal results. <u>His</u> <u>death</u> <u>launches</u> the final tragedy of the play.

Tybalt

> *What, drawn and talk of peace? I hate the word,*
> *As I hate hell, all Montagues, and thee.*

Tybalt is the only member of the Capulet and Montague families whose words and actions show the <u>ferocity</u> <u>and</u> <u>deep</u> <u>hatred</u> associated with the feud: he <u>attacks</u> <u>the</u> <u>peacemaker</u> Benvolio in the first brawl, he attempts to <u>challenge</u> Romeo at the feast and, of course, his final conflict with Mercutio and Romeo is a <u>pivotal</u> <u>point</u> <u>in</u> <u>the</u> <u>tragedy</u>. Remember, though, that Tybalt is also spoken of with affection by Juliet and the Nurse.

Benvolio

> *I do but keep the peace.*

Benvolio is a <u>peacemaker</u> and a <u>contrast</u> <u>to</u> <u>the</u> <u>aggressive</u> <u>Tybalt</u>. He is <u>cautious</u>, unlike Romeo. His word is <u>trusted</u> by both Montague and the Prince. He seems to be used as a contrast to the other characters in order to bring out their main features more clearly.

Lord Capulet

Capulet is a difficult character to assess because his behaviour seems so <u>contradictory</u>. He is a wealthy man who has married a woman much younger than himself, as she keeps reminding him. He presents an angry figure of <u>short-tempered</u> <u>authority</u> when

Juliet refuses to obey him, but at other times speaks to her <u>lovingly</u>. He appears to think Juliet is too young to marry and tries to put Paris off when he asks for her hand. However, later he suddenly agrees to the marriage and even <u>brings</u> <u>the</u> <u>date</u> <u>forward</u>, with disastrous results. He <u>rages</u> at Juliet when she shows reluctance to marry Paris, and embodies the conventional, <u>unfeeling</u> <u>world</u> in which the lovers find themselves. Only at the end of the play, when he mourns for his daughter's death, does he seem a sympathetic character once more.

Lady Capulet

Lady Capulet has married a much older, wealthy man. She seems to think of <u>marriage</u> <u>as</u> <u>a</u> <u>business</u> which must be carefully planned to be profitable. She is <u>unsympathetic</u> and vindictive when she demands that Tybalt's killer be put to death. Lady Capulet does not seem to have a particularly <u>affectionate</u> <u>relationship</u> with her daughter, but leaves her to the Nurse. When Juliet appeals to her mother not to cast her out, her appeal falls on deaf ears.

Paris

Paris is a character who is only lightly sketched in the play but who has an important role. He is an <u>honourable</u> <u>man</u> whose appearance helps to trigger the final tragedy. He <u>confidently</u> <u>assumes</u> that he will marry Juliet because this is the arrangement with her father, Capulet. He is the embodiment of the <u>predictable</u> <u>and</u> <u>conventional</u> <u>lover</u>. At the end of the play this <u>well-meaning</u> man speaks delicate words of grief for the girl he hardly knew. It is his <u>sense</u> <u>of</u> <u>honour</u>, rather than any feelings of jealousy, that provokes outrage in him when he thinks Romeo has come to desecrate her tomb. He dies in the fight with Romeo <u>without</u> <u>ever</u> <u>understanding</u> <u>the</u> <u>real</u> <u>situation</u>.

The Montagues

Montague and his wife remain thinly characterised and occupy predictable roles. Montague wishes to join in the first brawl, his wife dissuades him, then they make concerned enquiries about their melancholy son. Later, they reflect the mood of the play by defending Romeo (very briefly) after the death of Tybalt and by sharing the grief at the end of the play, Lady Montague so acutely that she dies. Montague then joins in the final atonement and reconciliation. Overall they appear less quarrelsome than the Capulets, and Montague's language is more restrained. They show warm affection towards Romeo, unlike the cold, harsh attitude that the Capulets show towards Juliet.

Escalus, Prince of Verona

The Prince is a symbol of order and peace. He is an important figure because much of the play is about the clash between love and hate, youth and age, life and death. He speaks out against the family feud but is unable to stop it. In the end he admits that he should have been firmer, because it is the death of the lovers and not his authority that finally brings peace. He too suffers because of the feud, and loses two of his kinsmen because of it.

About the author

William Shakespeare

William Shakespeare was born in Stratford-upon-Avon on 23 April 1564. His father, John Shakespeare, was a glove-maker by trade and a respected member of the community, holding, at various times, several important public offices, including those of councillor, Justice of the Peace and, in 1568, Mayor. Besides his craft as a glove-maker, he was a successful businessman trading in wool and involved in money lending. Shakespeare's mother, Mary Arden, was the daughter of a wealthy local farmer.

It is likely that, as the son of an important townsman, Shakespeare's education began at the town's 'petty' or junior school, before he went on to Stratford Grammar School, where he learned Latin and studied the classical writers, such as the Roman writers Ovid and Plautus. The influence of these writers can be seen in some of Shakespeare's plays, such as *Antony and Cleopatra* and *Julius Caesar*.

In 1582, when he was 18, Shakespeare married Anne Hathaway, the 26-year-old daughter of a local farmer. Their first child, Susanna, was born the following May and the twins, Judith and Hamnet, were born two years later. Sadly, though, Hamnet died in 1596 at the age of 11.

Very little is known about Shakespeare's life between 1585 and 1592, and these are sometimes known as 'The Lost Years'. We do know, however, that by 1592 he had moved to London. He probably left Stratford around 1586–7, and it seems likely that he joined one of the London-based theatre companies which sometimes visited the town. He would have known that London was the place to be if he wanted to become a successful actor/playwright. By 1592, Shakespeare had established his reputation as an actor and dramatist and was sufficiently well known to attract comment from some other dramatists of the time.

In 1593 all the theatres were closed because of the plague, and when they reopened the following year, Shakespeare had joined others to form a new theatre company under the patronage of the Lord Chamberlain, called The Lord Chamberlain's Men. Shakespeare wrote plays for this company for almost twenty years, and its leading actor, Richard Burbage, played many of the roles created by Shakespeare, such as Hamlet, Othello and King Lear.

In 1599 the Lord Chamberlain's Men built a new theatre, The Globe, on the south bank of the River Thames at Southwark, and Shakespeare was a major shareholder in this venture. In 1603, Elizabeth I died and James I (James IV of Scotland) came to the throne. Shakespeare's company changed its name to The King's Men, and in 1609 the company acquired another theatre, the Blackfriars, in addition to the Globe.

Shakespeare's success had made him a wealthy man, and as early as 1597 he had bought one of the biggest houses in Stratford – he kept close links with his home town even though he lived in London. Shakespeare's father had been granted a coat of arms in 1596, and after his father's death in 1601 Shakespeare inherited this and the rights of a gentleman, an unusual privilege for an actor or dramatist at the time.

During the early 1600s Shakespeare wrote some of his most famous tragedies including *Hamlet*, *Othello*, *King Lear* and *Macbeth*. His last plays, sometimes called the Romances, which include *Cymbeline*, The *Tempest* and *The Winter's Tale*, were written between about 1608 and 1612. About 1611 Shakespeare seems to have left London and retired to Stratford a wealthy man, though he kept up his connection with London as he was involved in a legal dispute over the Blackfriars theatre in 1615. He died in Stratford on 23 April 1616 and was buried there in the Holy Trinity Church.

Baz Luhrmann's 1996 film adaptation

In Elizabethan England, theatre-going was very popular and, although the theatres themselves were in London, travelling theatre companies went round the country and were hired by those who wanted a play to be performed as an attraction. Often plays were performed in temporary theatres created in inn yards, as well as at court and in the country houses of the wealthy. The plays, therefore, were seen by a wide range of people from all kinds of social backgrounds.

By the end of the 16th century, theatre-going was well established in England, but the theatres of Shakespeare's time were very different from modern theatres. The majority of them, such as The Globe in Southwark, London, were open-air and, as there was no artificial lighting, the plays had to be performed in daylight, normally in the afternoons. The theatre itself was round or hexagonal in shape, and there was a raised platform that jutted out into the audience. There was a recess at the back of the stage, which was supported by pillars and roofed to form a kind of turret from which a trumpeter signalled the beginning of the play and from which a flag flew, indicating that a performance was in progress.

The stage had no curtain and the main part of the audience stood around it on three sides. This section of the audience was called the 'groundlings'. A few special members of the audience were allowed to sit on the stage itself. In the galleries looking down on the stage and the groundlings, seating was provided for those who paid more to watch the play. These were covered and so afforded protection from the weather.

At the back of the stage, a large tapestry or curtain was hung concealing a recess and openings at either side from which the actors could enter and exit. The hanging might be colourful or dark, depending on the mood of the play. The stage itself was covered by a canopy, which rested on posts or pillars at either side. There was one or more trap doors in the stage itself, through which actors could quickly appear or disappear when necessary, for example in the appearance or disappearance of a ghost.

Behind the stage there were rooms called 'tiring rooms', in which the actors dressed and stored their various items and such props as were used. Although 'costumes' as such were not used, and actors dressed in the fashions of the times, these clothes were often more colourful or ornate and striking than those worn for everyday living. Painted scenery was not used, although props such as tables, chairs, thrones, cauldrons, swords, daggers and so on were used. All the female roles were played by men, as women were not allowed on the stage in Shakespeare's time, so tall boys with high-pitched voices were often trained to take women's parts.

People saw the theatre not only as a place to watch and enjoy a play, but as an opportunity to meet friends, exchange gossip and eat and drink. During performances, beer was often drunk and vendors moved among the groundlings selling various foods and sweetmeats. Elizabethan audiences were appreciative of a good play performed well but, if the play or performance was poor, they would often shout out derogatory remarks, make jokes at the actors' expense and throw things onto the stage – behaviour that is rarely seen in the modern-day theatre.

The feud

The play is full of examples of different kinds of conflict and disorder, and the feud between the Capulets and the Montagues is at the centre of the much of it. The feud is also the ultimate cause of all the deaths in the play and Shakespeare shows, through its consequences, its futility. We are made aware of this feud right from the outset of the play and it is the first thing that the Prologue mentions: 'Two households, both alike in dignity / In fair Verona where we lay our scene, / From ancient grudge break to new mutiny, / Where civil blood makes hands unclean…'.

The opening scene of the play itself emphasises this feud and the disorder it causes in Verona, creating a situation so serious that the Prince threatens death to anyone who disturbs the peace of the city again because of it. The love of Romeo and Juliet is, therefore, set within the context of hate generated by the feud and in that sense the feud is directly responsible for the tragedy that ensues. The hatred that it sets up is in direct conrast to the love of Romeo and Juliet, and in the end they are the victims of it, as the Prince points out at the end of the play: 'See what a scourge is laid upon your hate! / That heaven finds means to kill your joys with love…' (Act 5 Sc 3).

Fate and fortune

Fate and fortune are an important theme in the play. From the very start, the sense that Romeo and Juliet's lives are controlled by fate and that they are destined to suffer tragic consequences is made clear in the Prologue, where they are described as 'star-crossed lovers'. Before leaving to go to the Capulet ball where he meets Juliet for the first time, Romeo says he feels his future is 'hanging in the stars', and towards the end of the play when he hears of Juliet's death he says that he is 'fortune's fool'. The overall structure of the play and the way the story unfolds produces a feeling of inevitability about the ending, and everything that can go wrong for the lovers does go wrong. The accidental death of Mercutio sparks off a chain of events which leads to the death of Tybalt and in turn to the banishment of Romeo. Capulet's decision that Juliet must marry Paris puts her under pressure to find a way out. Her father's unexpected decision to bring the marriage forward increases this still further. Finally, the failed delivery of the friar's letter, and his own late arrival at the tomb, seals the lover's fate.

Light and dark

Images of darkness in the play stand for death, violence, sadness and secrecy. At the start of the play Romeo seeks out darkness because he is sad and depressed. Later on he and Juliet welcome the night because then they can safely be alone in secret. At the end of the play the blackness of the tomb and the dark night outside emphasise the sadness and tragedy of the lovers' deaths.

Images of light, whiteness or paleness in the play often appear in connection with ideas of love, life and hope. Romeo describes Juliet as being like the sun, brighter than the light of a torch or the stars. Juliet talks about Romeo's love being pure – whiter than snow. Even in the darkness of the tomb at the end of the play Romeo says that Juliet's beauty makes the darkness light.

Love

Love is an important theme in the play and appears in many forms. Different characters talk about love from very different points of view. At the start the servants Sampson and Gregory see love as brutish and crude. Romeo's early sadness is a kind of intellectual love – he is in love with the idea of being in love. Mercutio and the Nurse talk about love from a very physical, bawdy point of view. At the other extreme, Lord and Lady Capulet see love merely as a financial transaction to do with securing and retaining wealth. The love between Romeo and Juliet is deep and passionate and is more powerful than hatred and even death.

Time

Time and the sense of time passing too quickly are ideas that are often repeated in the play. The speed with which events happen is an important factor in the tragedy. At first time passes slowly, as Romeo frets about Rosaline and complains that the hours are long. Later Capulet complains that the years rush past too quickly. Romeo compares Juliet with a winged messenger of heaven, but Juliet worries that their love is too sudden and rash. The Friar complains that the lovers are in too much of a hurry. The message about the Friar's plan is delayed, and Friar Lawrence himself arrives at the end just seconds too late to stop the final tragedy. The whole play seems hurried. Characters rush into marriage, Romeo is banished for an impulsive action, Capulet cannot wait to get Juliet married to Paris. The play is filled with speed – speed to kill whoever is in the way and speed to commit suicide when life seems empty.

Religion

Many images in the play stem from the religious ideas of Shakespeare's time, and there are many examples of a 'religious' vocabulary in the play, through the use of words such as 'heaven', 'mass', 'angel' and 'God'. Romeo and Juliet's first conversation makes use of an extended image in which Romeo compares Juliet to a shrine or a saint, thus emphasising the spirituality of their love: 'If I profane with my unworthiest hand, / This holy shrine, the gentle sin is this, / My lips two blushing pilgrims ready stand, / To sooth the rough touch with a tender kiss.' (Act 1 Sc 5).

Friar Lawrence adds a further religious aspect to the play, and his actions in many ways raise questions when judged against the actions you would expect from a 'man of God'. Set against the religious elements of the play, the suicide of Romeo and Juliet has an even greater impact.

Death

Love is a central concern of Romeo and Juliet, but death is equally important in the play. Five characters die in the course of the action, but the preoccupation with death runs through much of the language of the play. At several points Juliet is presented as 'Death's bride', for example when she hears of Romeo's banishment, she says that 'death not Romeo, take my maidenhead.' (Act 3 Sc 2), and later, when Juliet refuses to marry Paris, her mother says of her, 'I would the fool were married to her grave.' (Act 3 Sc 5) When it appears that Juliet is dead, Capulet remarks, 'Death is my son-in-law, Death is my heir, / My daughter he hath wedded.' (Act 4 Sc 5). When Romeo finds Juliet's body in the Capulet vault, he too uses the personification of Death to describe her: 'Death that hath sucked the honey of thy breath, / Hath had no power yet upon thy beauty...' (Act 5 Sc 3), and he goes on, 'Shall I believe / That unsubstantial Death is amorous, / And that the lean abhorred monster keeps / Thee here in dark to be his paramour?'

This may seem a morbid fascination to a modern audience, but the Elizabethans, with an average life expectancy much lower than that of today, were much more conscious of their mortality.

Text commentary

Act I

Prologue

> **❝** *A pair of star-cross'd lovers, take their life* **❞**

The <u>Prologue</u> features a device from ancient Greek drama (the Chorus) which Shakespeare uses rarely. The Greek Chorus was used to comment on the events in the play; here it gives the audience the facts of the feud and how the <u>deaths</u> <u>of</u> <u>the</u> <u>lovers</u> will end it. The ending is deliberately revealed so that the audience may judge characters and events in the light of the final tragedy and also to intensify the <u>tragedy</u> by making it seem inevitable. The Chorus emphasises that <u>the</u> <u>lovers</u> <u>are</u> <u>fated</u>. They are '<u>star-cross'd</u>', their love is '<u>death-marked</u>' and they are born of their parents' '<u>fatal</u> <u>loins</u>'.

Scene 1

> **❝** *Have at thee coward.* **❞**

The play starts like a comedy, with <u>word-play</u> <u>and</u> <u>puns</u> from the two servants Gregory and Sampson, although they are armed and <u>ready</u> <u>for</u> <u>trouble</u>. Notice Sampson's one-dimensional idea of <u>love</u> as a kind of rape fantasy. He thinks love is just a matter of the brutal conquest of another's body, a matter of 'cutting off' a woman's virginity, and his <u>imagery</u> about the <u>human</u> <u>body</u> reflects this – it is <u>vulgar</u> and <u>crude</u>. For Sampson, even love has become a kind of hate.

Explore

Explain the puns used in this opening section.

Text commentary

References to 'naked weapon' and 'tool' emphasise the physical side of love, as do other references to striking and thrusting. Amidst a whirl of this kind of talk, Sampson and Gregory meet their deadly enemies. The speed with which fighting breaks out prepares the audience for the way haste and speed play a big part in the coming tragedy. Many characters in the play seem to act first and think later. This quarrel begins almost as a farce; biting your thumb at someone is an ancient Italian insult.

> **❝Turn thee Benvolio, look upon thy death.❞**

'Benvolio' means 'good will' and, true to his name he tries to stop the fight. When Tybalt arrives, though, he is in characteristically aggressive mood. Tybalt's name comes from the old story of Reynard the Fox, where Tybert is a cat (see also Act 2 Sc 4). Tybalt seems to hate hell, peace, Montagues – everything. His character never changes. He is always excitable and angry and eager to fight.

Explore

What impression do the heads of the two families make on their first appearance? Do you think they seem dangerous, or foolish, or both?

Capulet and Montague go through the motions of joining in the fight. Notice how Lady Capulet deflates her foolish husband – he calls for his sword and she suggests he'd be better off with a crutch. Lady Montague restrains her husband too, by holding on to him and scolding him.

> **❝Rebellious subjects, enemies of peace❞**

Escalus is furious with both families. He compares their behaviour to that of beasts. He says that there have already been three brawls and he has had enough. He is angry because their pointless fighting is disrupting the social life of the city and he threatens death to anyone who fights again.

"*O where is Romeo? Saw you him today?*"

Characters have appeared in a careful order up to this point in the play. You have met Capulet's servants, Montague's servants, Benvolio, Tybalt, the Capulets, the Montagues and then the Prince. The <u>scene</u> <u>is</u> <u>set</u> for the <u>two</u> <u>main</u> <u>characters</u> who have yet to appear.

Benvolio becomes <u>poetic</u> when he talks about Romeo. Notice how the <u>atmosphere</u> <u>of</u> <u>conflict</u> suddenly <u>disappears</u> as Romeo is mentioned. Benvolio talks about sunlight, secrets and silence. These ideas and <u>images</u> accompany Romeo and Juliet throughout the play and you should keep an eye out for the consistent way they are used by Shakespeare to <u>create</u> <u>a</u> <u>deliberate</u> <u>mood</u> or <u>atmosphere</u> around the lovers.

Explore

Keep a log of the puns used in the play as you come across them.

Benvolio says that Romeo has been walking underneath a grove of sycamore trees. The name is probably being used as a <u>pun</u>: 'sick amour'.

Romeo seeks out the darkness in his sadness. He is talked of as a <u>fleeting</u> <u>shadow</u> and is already being associated with <u>speed</u> <u>and</u> <u>quickness</u>.

"*What sadness lengthens Romeo's hours?*"

In Romeo's first long speech he talks about how <u>love</u> <u>and</u> <u>hate</u> have become <u>mixed</u> <u>together</u>, so that nothing is clear any more. Romeo's <u>emotional</u> and <u>mental</u> <u>confusion</u> is brought out in a series of <u>oxymorons</u>, that is to say, phrases made up of <u>opposites</u>. To begin with he talks of 'brawling love' and 'loving hate'. See how many more oxymorons you can find in this speech. These images of <u>chaos</u> and <u>confusion</u> are repeated often throughout the play, where <u>life</u> is seen as <u>death</u> and death as life. Just as the world of Verona is chaotic and confused because of the feuding families, so Romeo is <u>confused</u> because his feelings are in <u>turmoil</u>.

Romeo's language is <u>artificial</u>, intellectual and rather forced. He uses so many <u>ornate</u> and different descriptions for his feelings because he is not really in love at all – he is <u>in</u> <u>love</u> <u>with</u> <u>the</u> <u>idea</u> <u>of</u> <u>being</u> <u>in</u> <u>love</u>. He uses many <u>rhyming</u> <u>couplets</u>, which makes what he says sound more like a well-rehearsed speech than a true expression of emotional torment. Later when he meets Juliet, you will see how his language becomes more <u>sincere</u> <u>and</u> <u>passionate</u>. Romeo seems almost desperate to fall in love, but it is an <u>idealised</u> kind of love he wants; he is <u>unrealistic</u>, uncompromising and given to extremes, which helps to prepare us for his headlong fall into <u>passionate</u> <u>love</u> with Juliet.

Explore

Oxymoron is a compressed form of antithesis, where words with opposite meanings are combined in a phrase, e.g. 'O heavy lightness'.

Act 1 Scene 2

❝*But woo her gentle Paris, get her heart*❞

The plot begins to develop some twists here. Paris wants to marry Juliet and this will produce <u>tragic</u> <u>complications</u> for her relationship with Romeo. Paris, unlike Romeo, is <u>calm</u> and <u>even-tempered</u>. Because of the family feud, Romeo cannot of course speak to Capulet when he falls in love with Juliet. Notice Paris's attitude to love – that a woman is fulfilled not by passion but by the calmer pleasures of motherhood.

Juliet's 'ripeness' to be a bride is talked of in the same breath as summer 'withering'. Elsewhere, Montague talks about Romeo being blighted like a bud bitten by a worm. These hints in the <u>imagery</u> <u>prepare</u> <u>you</u> <u>for</u> <u>the</u> <u>tragedy</u> <u>to</u> <u>come</u>. The love of Romeo and Juliet is full of promise and <u>hope</u> <u>for</u> <u>the</u> <u>future</u> but it will be <u>blighted</u> and <u>doomed</u> <u>by</u> <u>fate</u>. Capulet's other children have all died and the earth has 'swallowed' them. This is another example of the imagery of <u>death's</u> <u>mouth</u> (the tomb) in the play, which reminds you of the ever-present idea of the <u>lovers</u> <u>as</u> <u>'star-crossed'</u> <u>or</u> <u>fated</u>.

Capulet says that at his banquet that night there will be many lovely young women – 'earth-treading stars'. This connection between heavenly things and events on earth was a common idea in Shakespeare's time, and it is another example of the images of <u>light</u> <u>and</u> <u>love</u> being brought together.

❝*come and crush a cup of wine* **❞**

Explore

See what examples you can find of this use of humour in the short speech before the entry of Romeo and Benvolio. Here you should note Peter scoring off Romeo by giving correct, but very limited, answers.

The comic servant, Peter, cannot read and so must get help to obey his master's instructions to find the people written on the list. Peter is described in the cast list as 'a clown' which means that the part was originally played by a member of the company who specialised in clowning and always played such parts. Though this is a very small part, we can find examples of typical <u>clownish</u> <u>humour</u>. One element of the humour is nonsense, muddling things in an illogical pattern.

Romeo and Benvolio speak to each other in <u>verse</u> while the servant speaks in <u>prose</u>, as fits his lower status. Notice that noble characters use prose when speaking to, or about 'lower' things.

Romeo uses the idea of light and seeing by saying that the 'all-seeing sun' never saw a beauty to match Rosaline. Later in the play – in Act 2 Sc 2 – Romeo again uses the imagery of light and seeing to <u>describe</u> <u>his</u> <u>love</u> for Juliet, but she rejects it. Juliet says the light of the moon is not constant and their love may be more like <u>a</u> <u>brief</u> <u>sudden</u> <u>flash</u> <u>of</u> <u>lightning</u>. Notice how the speeches are full of references to <u>light,</u> <u>burning,</u> <u>crystals,</u> <u>shining,</u> <u>eyes</u> and <u>looking</u>. This continuous use of related images is part of the <u>structure</u> of the play and binds the different parts together.

Act 1 Scene 3

> **"Go girl, seek happy nights to happy days."**

Explore

As you work through the play, make a note of the different kinds of speech spoken by different characters.

Scenes 1 and 2 are about the world of men; scene 3 concentrates on the world as it affects women. The Nurse is informal and natural in her manner and speech, while Lady Capulet seems formal, abrupt and somewhat artificial. As with Romeo, Benvolio and the servant in the previous scene, the difference between the 'high' status of Lady Capulet and the 'low' one of the Nurse is reflected in the content and style of their speech.

The Nurse's long speech here covers the whole life of the human body from Juliet's childhood to her own old age. The Nurse was Juliet's wet-nurse and she tells us how she persuaded the baby to give up feeding at the breast by rubbing wormwood (a bitter plant) on her nipples. The Nurse's daughter Susan died young and Juliet has in many ways replaced her in the Nurse's affections. Ironically, Juliet will also be 'too good for' the Nurse and this brief reference is ominous in the same way as Montague's earlier images of cankered buds. The Nurse has obviously had a long and close relationship with Juliet, which explains why Lady Capulet calls her back to join in the discussion about her proposed marriage to Paris.

> **"Thou wilt fall backward when thou comest of age"**

The Nurse's bawdy jokes and her emphasis on physical lust act as an important balance to the later idealised and innocent love of Romeo and Juliet and to the formal and rather artificial love of Paris. Just as the Nurse is a balance to Juliet, so is Mercutio to Romeo. The whole of this amusing scene, in which the chatty and rambling Nurse keeps irritating Lady Capulet, is a temporary diversion from the tragedy

Explore

Notice how Shakespeare intersperses the serious action with scenes that give light relief at various points. Make a note of where these scene come in the play.

to come. Scenes like this are <u>'light relief'</u> from the impending disaster and actually help to <u>build tension</u> because, while they seem to be about other things, they contain lots of <u>cross-references</u> to the main imagery and action. For example, Juliet is associated with 'falling backwards' (into physical love) and the matter of her possible marriage to Paris is raised.

> ❝*The valiant Paris seeks you for his love*❞

In keeping with her character in the rest of the play, Lady Capulet introduces the topic of marriage to Paris very abruptly and <u>without much sensitivity</u>. She expects Juliet to commit herself to someone she has not yet seen. Lady Capulet says Juliet could 'share all that he doth possess' and seems to see marriage as a <u>sharing of position and wealth</u> rather than a <u>sharing of love</u>. The Nurse agrees that Juliet could 'grow' by marrying Paris, but as usual has in mind a more physical meaning than Lady Capulet's!

Act 1 Scene 4

> ❝*my mind misgives*❞

Romeo's friends indulge in <u>word-play</u> about his love, saying that he should not be sad. Romeo is 'heavy' with sadness and has a 'soul of lead'; he has been pierced with Cupid's arrow. Although Romeo's bookish sadness will soon be lifted, his love for Juliet eventually brings more sadness by the end of the play.

> ❝*Peace, peace Mercutio, peace.*
> *Thou talk'st of nothing.*❞

Mercutio is <u>wild and fiery, volatile</u> and <u>impulsive</u>. His <u>words</u> run away with him in an almost <u>uncontrollable flow</u> and, in Act 2

Sc 4, Romeo says that Mercutio 'will speak more in a minute than he will stand to in a month'. The notion of romantic love <u>amuses</u> Mercutio, who has a much more <u>basic</u> and <u>down-to-earth</u> view of love which revolves around <u>physical</u> <u>passion</u>.

Explore

What kind of view of the world do you think Mercutio has? Cynical, romantic, realistic, amused, contemptuous?

Mercutio says that dreams are inhabited by the Fairy Queen Mab and that Romeo seems to have been enchanted by her. The dreams which Mercutio talks about are full of <u>bizarre</u> <u>examples</u> of wishful thinking: 'vain fantasies' as he calls them; Queen Mab drives her fairy coach through lovers' brains so that they dream of love, over ladies' lips so that they dream of kisses, over soldiers' necks so that they dream of cutting throats. In such dreams reality and madness seem to meet, and it is this sort of lovers' dream that is about to come true for Romeo.

Romeo seems to <u>foresee</u> his own death here, a 'consequence yet hanging in the stars' as he calls it. He calls upon the one 'that hath the steerage' of his 'course' – he who guides the path of his life – to direct him safely. The sea is often used by Shakespeare as a symbol of the powerful and unpredictable <u>forces</u> <u>of</u> <u>fate</u> and the audience already knows that Romeo's <u>fate</u> <u>is</u> <u>fixed</u>, for he is 'star-cross'd'. This scene ends with a sense of <u>foreboding</u>, but Shakespeare uses the opening of the following scene to relieve the tension.

Explore

There are many references to fate and fortune in the play. Make a note of them as you find them.

Act 1 Scene 5

The previous scene ended on a gloomy and threatening note, with Romeo having a premonition of his death. The opening of this scene is concerned with <u>everyday</u> <u>domestic</u> <u>matters</u> as the servants joke among themselves while they clear up after dinner.

Text commentary

Capulet welcomes everybody and, although he is too old to dance himself, he encourages everybody else to join in because he likes to watch the young people enjoy themselves and wants his party to be a success. His speech is full of references to walking and dancing, and <u>contrasts</u> the hot vigour of <u>youth</u> with the sedateness of <u>age</u> and its confusions.

> **❝ O she doth teach the torches to burn bright ❞**

Romeo sees Juliet and is <u>stunned</u> by her beauty. He associates her with <u>glowing light</u>, says she shines like a rich jewel, compares her to a snowy dove among crows and says she is 'blessed'. As Benvolio said he would, Romeo now forswears his love for Rosaline at once. Near the start of Sc 2, Benvolio advised Romeo that, since one fire burns out another and one pain is made less by the anguish of another, he should therefore find a new love. This now happens, <u>but</u> <u>we</u> <u>know</u> that Romeo's pain will be made greater, not less, by his love for Juliet.

Explore

There are many views of love. Do you think love at first sight really exists? What are the signs of falling in love?

You will notice in the rest of the play how Romeo often talks about Juliet in terms of <u>shining light, whiteness</u> and <u>purity</u>, and as having <u>holy qualities</u>. He also says here that Juliet has beauty that is 'too rich for use' and is 'for earth too dear', meaning that she is too fine for the uses of this world and too precious to be on earth. This sounds rather <u>ominous</u> and again <u>reinforces the sense of foreboding</u>.

> **❝ Tis he, that villain Romeo ❞**

In <u>contrast</u> to Romeo's <u>gentle</u> and <u>admiring</u> love speech, Tybalt arrives, as usual <u>spoiling for a fight</u>. Capulet's banquet is a masked ball, so all the guests wear fancy masks to <u>conceal their identity</u>. Tybalt recognises Romeo's voice. He is <u>furious</u> that a

Text commentary

Montague should intrude into their party and says he will fight Romeo for this insult. Capulet tells him to calm down because Romeo is known to be <u>virtuous</u> and <u>well-behaved</u>. When Tybalt persists in <u>wanting to kill</u> Romeo because he is a Montague, Capulet becomes furious at his disobedience.

❝My lips two blushing pilgrims ready stand❞

Romeo and Juliet's speeches to each other are full of <u>religious</u> <u>overtones</u>, yet the bulk of what they say concerns the human body. Although they talk of lips and hands kissing and touching, and actually kiss each other, they also talk about holy shrines, gentle sins, pilgrims, devotion, saints and prayers. Their <u>formal</u> use of language has a <u>dignified</u> pace and stresses the <u>purity</u> and <u>sincerity</u> of their love for each other. Romeo's language is still a little forced and <u>exaggerated</u> and he has not yet completely shaken off his somewhat studied manner – Juliet says he kisses by the book rather than from the heart. The duet between Romeo and Juliet is in <u>sonnet</u> <u>form</u> and its use of <u>religious words</u> <u>isolates</u> the characters from the rest of the scene and its bustling activity.

❝My only love sprung from my only hate❞

The Nurse brings a message that Juliet's mother wants her. Romeo is <u>stunned</u> to learn that Juliet is a Capulet, the family so <u>bitterly at odds</u> with his own. Juliet wants to know Romeo's name and asks the Nurse to find it out. She says that if she cannot marry Romeo she will die – another <u>ominous</u> comment. This is the first time in the play that death is portrayed as a bridegroom, although this image occurs again at the end. Juliet is <u>distraught</u> that she has found her only love within the family she has been <u>brought up to hate</u>.

Explore

It can be difficult to decide whether the play is more about hate or love, death or life. What do you think?

Quick quiz 1

Uncover the plot

Delete two of the three alternatives given, to find the correct plot

1   In Verona/Mantua/Rome, a fight between Montagues and Capulets is broken up by Benvolio/an Officer/the Prince.

2   Romeo tells Benvolio/Tybalt/Mercutio the cause of his sadness – his love for Juliet/Angelica/Rosaline.

3   Tybalt/Paris/Balthasar asks Capulet for Juliet's hand.

4   Lady Capulet/Lord Capulet/the Nurse tells Juliet about Paris.

5   Romeo meets Juliet and finds out that she is a Montague/Capulet.

6   Juliet feels that her 'only love' has 'sprung from a loathed enemy/a Capulet/my only hate'.

Who? What? When? Where? Why? How?

1   Who does Mercutio say gives dreams?

2   Who 'doth teach the torches to burn bright'?

3   What does Lady Capulet call for when Capulet calls for his sword?

4   What traditional Italian insult starts the brawl?

5   Where has Benvolio found Romeo walking before dawn?

6   Why (give three reasons) does Capulet restrain Tybalt at the feast?

7   How is Romeo recognised at the feast – and why is this the only way he can be recognised?

8   How many brawls have there already been between the families?

Who said that?

1   Who says: 'Part, fools, put up your swords, you know not what you do'?

2   Who says: 'bright smoke, cold fire, sick health'?

3   Who agrees: 'True, I talk of dreams, / Which are the children of an idle brain'?

4   Who calls Romeo 'a virtuous and well-govern'd youth'?

5   Who shouts: 'What, drawn, and talk of peace? I hate the word!'?

Act 2

Act 2 Prologue

66 *Alike bewitched by the charm of looks* 99

Again the Chorus is used to keep the audience up to date with the story by <u>summarising</u> what has happened and by telling how the lovers' passion 'lends them power' to meet in the coming scenes, despite being enemies.

The Chorus speaks the third sonnet in the play, having started the play with the first. The second sonnet is spoken by Romeo and Juliet when they first meet.

Act 2 Scene 1

66 *Blind is his love, and best befits the dark.* 99

xplore

nink about Mercutio's ttitude towards love. ow does his view of ve differ from omeo's?

Mercutio calls for Romeo, making <u>bawdy</u> <u>fun</u> <u>of</u> <u>him</u> because he is in love with Rosaline. Mercutio and his friends do not yet know that Romeo has met Juliet. Benvolio says that Romeo will be <u>angry</u> at being mocked this way.

Mercutio talks about Cupid and Venus, two pagan <u>symbols</u> <u>of</u> <u>love</u>, but speaks about love in the most physical of terms, referring to Rosaline's 'scarlet lip' and 'quivering thigh'. Mercutio always talks about the human body, as he did in his Queen Mab

speech, in very <u>physical</u> and <u>bawdy</u> <u>terms</u>. Here he says that Romeo will sit under a medlar tree. This is a piece of coarse Elizabethan slang; the medlar fruit, like a small brown apple, was said to resemble the female sex organs. This is why Mercutio says Romeo will think of Rosaline in these terms, because love for Mercutio is the same as physical lust. He and many other characters in the play <u>cannot</u> <u>understand</u> that love can be <u>pure</u> and <u>passionate</u>.

Act 2 Scene 2

Romeo, who has heard the conversation between Benvolio and Mercutio, remarks that Mercutio can easily <u>make</u> <u>fun</u> of him because Mercutio has never been in love: 'he jests at scars that never felt a wound'. The way in which Romeo expresses this is unintentionally <u>ironic</u>, because Mercutio is soon to be scarred and fatally wounded in his fight with Tybalt.

The play is full of commotion and activity. Very rarely do we find a scene set in stillness: here, perhaps briefly at the start of Act 3 Sc 5 and, of course, finally in the silence of the tomb. <u>Imagery</u> <u>of</u> <u>light</u> and <u>seeing</u> is important in this scene. Romeo's love for Juliet is often expressed in terms of <u>light</u> <u>shining</u> <u>within</u> <u>the</u> <u>darkness</u>. Light imagery reaches its climax in this love scene, when he says that she is the <u>source</u> <u>of</u> <u>all</u> <u>light,</u> <u>the</u> <u>sun</u>.

Romeo connects the <u>pale</u> <u>moonlight</u> with <u>sickness</u> and <u>grief</u> and says that only fools have anything to do with it. This echoes the 'sick amour' he experienced at the start of the play when he was foolishly in love with Rosaline. He says the moon is 'envious' of the light of the sun and is 'sick and green'. Romeo's speech in praise of Juliet describes the <u>beauty</u> <u>of</u> <u>the</u> <u>light</u> <u>of</u> <u>the</u> <u>sun</u> <u>and</u> <u>the</u> <u>other</u> <u>stars</u>. Later, he speaks of her as a 'bright angel' who, as a 'winged messenger of heaven', is far above ordinary mortals on earth. Romeo again uses several <u>religious</u> <u>references</u> to describe Juliet, indicating the kind of love he feels for her.

> **❝O Romeo, Romeo, wherefore art thou Romeo?❞**

Juliet, unaware that Romeo is hiding below in the garden, says that <u>she</u> <u>does</u> <u>not</u> <u>care</u> that he is a <u>Montague</u>. She says that if a

rose were called by a different name it would still smell as sweet. Notice that Juliet uses an <u>image</u> of a <u>beautiful flower</u> to talk about Romeo. Her description of her ears drinking in his words shows that all her <u>senses</u> are awakened by her love for him and introduces <u>imagery of mouths, drinking</u>, etc.

For stony limits cannot hold love out

Explore

What is the dramatic effect of Juliet speaking while unaware of Romeo's presence?

Juliet is worried that Romeo risks death if he is discovered in her garden and wonders how he climbed the high orchard walls. He replies that love enabled him to climb the walls so easily. The 'stony limits' of Juliet's orchard, which Romeo says cannot hold out his love, also appear again at the end of the play, where they become the stony limits of the graveyard and the tomb. Romeo's love for Juliet becomes <u>so strong that not even death</u> can keep them apart. He says that love fears nothing, <u>preparing</u> us for the <u>desperate</u> measures which Juliet takes later to avoid marrying Paris.

thy kinsmen are no stop to me

Romeo unwittingly <u>foretells</u> his own death. He says he would rather have his life ended quickly by being found here in the garden by Juliet's kinsmen – 'ended by their hate', as he puts it – than die of slow suffering <u>without Juliet's love</u>. Because the audience already knows how the story will end, this comment by Romeo is a piece of dramatic irony.

O swear not by the moon, th'inconstant moon

Romeo used imagery about light when describing his love for Rosaline and now he tries to <u>use the moon</u> to evoke his love for Juliet. Continuing her words about being truthful, she says she does not want him to swear by the 'inconstant' (changeable) moon. The moon's light is <u>not</u>

Explore

Think about the imagery that Romeo and Juliet use here. Write down and explain images that you find particularly effective.

constant because it waxes and wanes throughout the year – sometimes it is strong and at others it disappears.

Romeo is intoxicated by his passion for Juliet but she says 'it is too rash, too unadvis'd, too sudden', like the lightning in a storm. In a way Juliet is correct, because their love will indeed be like a brief wondrous flash of light in the darkness of the feud between their two families.

Juliet is afraid of being 'quickly won'. Time and the sense of time passing quickly are ideas that are repeated often in the play, where the action takes place in a very short space of time – this point, for example, marks the end of the first day.

Notice the imagery of growth in Juliet's words: their 'bud of love' may become a 'beauteous flower' when they next meet, if it is breathed upon by 'summer's ripening breath'. References to nature tell you that their love is as natural as the seasons, and as innocent and beautiful as a flowering bud. Notice that their love has not yet fully flowered and that the ending of the story will prevent this. Also, the natural development of bud to flower is completed in the natural cycle of death and decay and the play has already prepared us for this with images such as the worm in the bud (Act 1 Sc 1).

❝❝O blessed, blessed night❞❞

Explore

What do you think is the dramatic effect of Juliet's exits and entrances prompted by the Nurse's cries and her desire to speak to Romeo?

Romeo is afraid that his wonderful meeting with Juliet has been only a dream. Notice how it is she who returns with practical plans for seeing each other again and for arranging to be married.

She uses imagery of birds and flight – swiftness and flight will shortly become important in the action. Ominously, she also says that if Romeo were a bird she would kill him 'with much cherishing': dramatic irony again.

Act 2 Scene 3

> **❝** *Wisely and slow, they stumble that run fast.* **❞**

The Friar is the last of the important characters to appear. Much of his speech is in <u>rhyme</u> and, although rhyme is often used in the play, it is never used in such concentration as here. This helps set the Friar apart from the other characters.

Explore

Think about what the Friar says and does in this scene. What is your initial impression of him?

The Friar is introduced to us in this long speech which is in some ways equivalent to Mercutio's Queen Mab speech in Act 1 Sc 4. The Friar says the earth is both nature's <u>womb</u> and her <u>tomb</u> and that people are nature's children, who suck on her 'natural bosom', meaning that they are nourished by the natural world. He says that the plants he gathers contain reviving medicine as well as poison and that even the most vile things produce some good.

He also says that people are like plants and have both <u>good</u> <u>and</u> <u>evil</u> in them. The good in man he says is 'grace', meaning graciousness or divine virtue. The evil in man he says is 'rude will' meaning fleshly desire or uncontrolled passion. This idea, that too much will or <u>passion</u> can turn to vice, is an <u>underlying</u> <u>theme</u> in the play and one which the Friar is always repeating. Just as the Friar mentions <u>poison</u>, the future victim of poison, Romeo, enters.

> **❝** *We met, we wooed, and made exchange of vow* **❞**

Romeo says that he has been 'wounded' by Juliet but that the Friar has medicine ('physic') that can cure him. This is ironic because although Romeo means that he has fallen in love with Juliet and the Friar can marry them, in the end it is the Friar's potion for Juliet that has <u>disastrous</u>

consequences. Following on from the Friar, Romeo's speech combines the <u>imagery</u> <u>of</u> <u>food,</u> <u>love-sickness</u> and <u>medicine</u>.

The Friar is <u>amazed</u> that Romeo has fallen out of love and in again so quickly, but he agrees to help him

Act 2 Scene 4

> **66** *Alas poor Romeo, he is already dead* **99**

Mercutio believes that Romeo has stayed out all night because of his love-sickness for Rosaline. Benvolio says that Tybalt has written a letter challenging Romeo to a duel. Mercutio replies that Romeo is as <u>good</u> <u>as</u> <u>dead</u> already <u>through</u> <u>love</u> and in no state to fight. Ironically this is true, but not in the way Mercutio means

Here, Mercutio <u>ridicules</u> the new fashion for the Italian style of fencing that was much scorned in England at this time because of its precise, almost dance-like, technique. He says that such fencing is too much 'by th' book', like Romeo's kissing. <u>Fancy</u> <u>speech</u> or <u>manners</u> – or fencing as here – are again equated with <u>falseness</u> and <u>shallowness</u>.

> **66** *Here comes Romeo, here comes Romeo!* **99**

Explore

How do Mercutio's words and actions here compare with the impression you formed of his character in Act 1?

Mercutio greets Romeo's entrance with another bout of <u>bawdy</u> <u>punning</u> in which Romeo joins. The <u>comic</u> <u>elements</u> of this scene create a change of atmosphere from the last scene and a <u>contrast</u> with the next.

Mercutio and Benvolio make fun of the Nurse and Mercutio dominates the first half of this scene with Romeo, just as the Nurse dominates the second. Romeo's comment about

Mercutio after he has left ('...loves to hear himself talk...') applies equally to the Nurse, and in some ways she and Mercutio are parallel characters: they are both <u>bawdy and</u> <u>talkative</u> and they both see life and its pleasures in purely <u>physical</u> <u>terms</u>.

Explore

What is your impression of the character of the Nurse?

The comic conversation with the Nurse, who often speaks more than she listens, tells us how she is to help with the <u>elopement</u> by lowering a rope ladder from Juliet's room for Romeo. Romeo imparts his message to the Nurse with some difficulty. See how many examples you can find of the Nurse changing the subject, failing to listen to the end of an instruction or simply pursuing her own conversational interests. Her question about Romeo and rosemary beginning with a letter (followed by her confusion of 'r' and a dog growling) suggests her illiteracy.

> *Doth not rosemary and Romeo begin both with a letter?*

The Nurse here connects rosemary with Romeo and says that Juliet is fond of both. Later, after the discovery of Juliet's body, the Friar mentions rosemary in connection with Juliet. Later still the Nurse casts rosemary on the body of Juliet, as the flower of remembrance, and this reference would therefore have had a <u>threatening</u> ring for Elizabethan audiences.

Act 2 Scene 5

> *What says he of our marriage, what of that?*

Juliet is <u>anxious</u> to know why the Nurse has been so long. She says love's messengers should travel as fast as the sun flickers when clouds blow over it. This image <u>connects</u> the themes of <u>haste</u> and <u>light</u> and reminds us of Juliet's observation that some forms of love appear and disappear as quickly as lightning. This scene <u>emphasises</u>

another theme: the <u>contrast</u> between the <u>impatience</u> <u>of</u> <u>youth</u> and the <u>slowness</u> <u>of</u> <u>age</u>; the blood rushes to Juliet's cheeks but the Nurse has a headache and an aching back.

This scene between Juliet and the Nurse <u>parallels</u> the one in Act 2 Sc 3 between Romeo and the Friar. Both conversations show <u>youth</u> <u>contrasted</u> <u>with</u> <u>age</u>. The Friar's attitude makes him appear <u>wise</u> and <u>kindly</u>, but the Nurse is content for Juliet to be happy and shares the <u>anticipation</u> of the <u>sexual</u> <u>pleasures</u> of her wedding bed that night ('you shall bear the burden soon at night').

Act 2 Scene 6

❝*These violent delights have violent ends***❞**

The Friar delivers his usual lecture about how the <u>excess</u> of any <u>passion</u> will lead to <u>tragedy</u>. What he says is <u>prophetic</u>, considering what fate has in store for the two lovers. Notice his warning that 'violent delights have violent ends' and that they are like 'fire and powder' (meaning gunpowder) because when they meet they <u>destroy</u> each other: 'as they kiss consume'.

❝*Too swift arrives as tardy as too slow***❞**

By this confusing remark the Friar means that people should love <u>moderately</u>, not with too much haste and passion (too swiftly) nor with too little interest or emotion (too slow). This is true on two separate occasions in the play: first, when the Friar's message to Romeo is delayed and Romeo buys poison in his ignorance of the plan to fake Juliet's death; second, when Romeo arrives at the tomb before Juliet has awoken from her mock-death and takes the poison before the Friar arrives to tell him the truth.

Uncover the plot

Delete two of the three alternatives given, to find the correct plot.

1   Benvolio and Mercutio seek Romeo/Rosaline/Tybalt.

2   Juliet declares her love for Romeo, who reveals himself, saying: 'I'll take thee at thy word'/'Shall I hear more?'/'If my heart's dear love'.

3   Juliet is afraid that he will fall from the high wall/that her kinsmen will kill him/that he will get lost.

4   Benvolio/Mercutio/Tybalt has challenged Romeo to a duel.

5   Told the news of Romeo's proposal, Juliet jumps/blushes/faints.

6   The lovers meet at the church/the orchard/the Friar's cell.

Who? What? Where? When? Why? How?

1   Who is 'the courageous captain of compliments'?

2   Who is 'a gentleman... that loves to hear himself talk'?

3   What two solutions does Juliet see to the problem of Romeo's identity?

4   What 'cannot hold love out'?

5   What does 'wherefore' mean (as in 'wherefore art thou Romeo?')?

6   Where is Juliet supposed to be going when she leaves to marry Romeo?

7   Where does the 'balcony scene' take place?

8   Why has Friar Lawrence chided Romeo?

Who said that?

1   Who says: 'My bounty is as boundless as the sea, / My love as deep'?

2   Who says: 'The earth that's nature's mother is her tomb'?

3   Who says: 'The pox of such antic, lisping, affecting fantasticoes!'?

4   Who says: 'Then love-devouring death do what he dare. / It is enough I may but call her mine.'?

5   Who says: 'But you shall bear the burden soon at night'?

Act 3

Act 3 Scene 1

> ❝*For now these hot days, is the mad blood stirring*❞

This scene marks the final appearance of Mercutio. After this, our attention is concentrated only on Romeo and Juliet. Unusually for Shakespeare, Romeo and Juliet has no <u>sub-plot</u> at all, and the simple and clear storyline which results gives the play a <u>relentless</u> feeling.

This scene is a major turning-point in the play and it is appropriate that it should start with references to heat and passion.

As usual the <u>peace-loving</u> Benvolio is all for <u>caution</u>. He says to Mercutio that the day is too hot, members of the Capulet family are about and they should leave. Mercutio replies that this is poor advice coming from someone as hot-tempered as Benvolio. This is <u>comic</u> because the only person more inclined to fight than Mercutio is Tybalt, whereas Benvolio is a <u>natural</u> <u>peacemaker</u>.

> ❝*Tybalt, you rat-catcher, will you walk?*❞

The exchange of insults between Mercutio and Tybalt shows how <u>both</u> of them will <u>pick a fight</u> over nothing. Benvolio warns them that they are in a public place where 'all eyes gaze on us' but they seem not to care. In any case, Tybalt is more interested in quarrelling with Romeo, who enters at this point.

The <u>audience</u> knows that Romeo has <u>just married</u> Juliet. Because Juliet is Tybalt's cousin, Romeo will not fight someone who is now a member of his own family. Tybalt <u>does not know</u> any of this, of course, and so he can't understand why Romeo will not be provoked into a fight. Mercutio is <u>disgusted</u> at Romeo and thinks that he is submitting to Tybalt's insults in a shameful way.

66 *a plague a' both your houses* 99

Mercutio fights with Tybalt but is <u>fatally</u> <u>wounded</u> as Romeo steps between them to try to stop them. Mercutio's insults to Tybalt revolve around his name. The <u>animal</u> <u>imagery</u> of 'rat-catcher' and 'king of cats' is continued as Mercutio threatens to take one of Tybalt's 'nine lives', and becomes <u>ironic</u> as he describes his fatal wound as 'a scratch'. Even as he lies fatally wounded, Mercutio's <u>language</u> is full of <u>humour</u>. He says his wound is not as 'deep as a well' nor as 'wide as a church door', but it is enough. He is also talking about his own funeral and his burial. He punningly tells Romeo that if he asks for him tomorrow he will find him 'a grave man', meaning he will <u>not</u> <u>be</u> <u>making</u> <u>any</u> <u>more</u> <u>jokes</u> because he will be in his grave. Mercutio leaves the scene, cursing both 'houses' and wishing a <u>plague</u> on both <u>Capulets</u> and <u>Montagues</u>.

Explore

Think about how Mercutio comes to be fatally wounded by Tybalt. How might the actors performing this scene present Tybalt's stabbing of Mercutio? Is it an accident, or does Tybalt use Romeo's intervention to strike at Mercutio?

66 *O Romeo, Romeo, brave Mercutio is dead* 99

Romeo <u>blames</u> <u>himself</u> for his friend's death, so when Tybalt returns he vows to show 'fire-ey'd fury' towards him. Romeo and Tybalt fight, and <u>Tybalt</u> <u>is</u> <u>killed</u>. Benvolio says that Romeo must escape quickly before he is caught, otherwise he will be subject to the death penalty as Prince Escalus warned at the start of the play. Romeo exclaims he is 'fortune's fool', then leaves. Romeo sees the <u>trap</u> <u>he</u> <u>is</u> <u>caught</u> <u>in</u>. If he escapes, he must leave his wife Juliet. If he stays, he risks the death penalty for brawling in the streets. He has ended up losing his best friend Mercutio and killing his wife's cousin.

Explore

How does the part Romeo plays in Mercutio's death add to the sense of dramatic tension at this point?

66 *Immediately we do exile him hence* 99

Benvolio tells the Prince about the fight. Lady Capulet takes up the violent theme of the feud and demands that Romeo be put to death in punishment.

Explore

Check through the remaining scenes of the play to find out how much time Romeo and Juliet will spend together now that the death of Tybalt has ruined their hopes.

Now, as the action focuses even more strongly on the tragic love story, comedy virtually disappears from the play. Mercutio is dead and, after her betrayal of Juliet later in the act, the Nurse plays a much less important role. Tybalt is now dead and Benvolio disappears from the action. In this scene the ever-reliable Benvolio acts as a Chorus to clarify matters.

Act 3 Scene 2

66 *Tybalt is gone and Romeo banished* 99

Events begin to move more quickly now and, even as Romeo's banishment is still ringing in your ears, you meet Juliet here longing for Romeo. Putting two such different things together produces a powerful dramatic contrast. It is appropriate that Juliet's long soliloquy, spoken in beautiful poetry, should begin with images of galloping horses, fire and speed. She wants night to come quickly so that she can secretly meet Romeo.

The Nurse brings the news to Juliet, but the confusion in the Nurse's speech makes it difficult for Juliet to know at once what the bad news is. Juliet asks the Nurse 'what storm is this that blows so contrary?' because of the seeming contradictions in what the Nurse is saying.

In Act 2 Sc 5, just as here, an impatient soliloquy by Juliet is followed by an urgent message from the Nurse which takes a long time to deliver.

Explore

What similarities and differences can you find between the scenes? Look at Juliet's mood at first, the atmosphere of the scene with the Nurse, and the reasons why the Nurse takes so long conveying her meaning.

When Juliet is finally told about the events that have happened, she curses Romeo: 'O serpent heart, hid with a flowering face...'. This speech is filled with the contrasting use of opposites (oxymorons), like Romeo's speech at the start of the play ('bright smoke, cold fire'). Concentrated in both speeches you will find many of the references which are scattered throughout the rest of the play. Notice, for example, the use of creatures like the serpent, raven and wolf to suggest dark and dangerous qualities.

66 *Blister'd be thy tongue* 99

Explore

What other reasons can you find for Juliet's first response and for her change of mind? She gives at least three reasons in defence of Romeo.

Juliet's anger at the Nurse's criticism of Romeo shows her loyalty to Romeo and she quickly recovers from her initial reaction to Tybalt's death. Undoubtedly this change of attitude to Romeo is partly a reaction to the Nurse's words, 'Shame come to Romeo'.

Juliet's reaction to Romeo's banishment is significant. She says that Romeo's banishment has killed everything: 'father, mother, Tybalt, Romeo, Juliet' and that there 'is no end, no limit, measure, bound, in that word's death'. She says that this sad news has removed all joy from her life. Notice how she says that death, not Romeo, will take her maidenhead (her virginity). This idea is taken up again at the beginning of the next scene.

Act 3 Scene 3

66 *Hold thy desperate hand* 99

Romeo has hidden at Friar Lawrence's cell. The Friar comes to tell him that his punishment is not death but banishment. This is an ironic twist to the story because the audience knows that

this will be <u>reversed</u> at the end of the play. Notice how the Friar uses the <u>imagery</u> <u>of</u> <u>death</u> <u>as</u> <u>a</u> <u>lover</u>, which Juliet also used at the end of the last scene, when he says that Romeo is 'wedded to calamity'. This reinforces what the Chorus said about the lovers being '<u>star-cross'd</u>'. The image of death as a lover appears again more strongly in the tomb at the end of the play. The Friar tells Romeo that he should be patient and accept the sentence of Prince Escalus.

There is no world without Verona's walls

Romeo says that to be banished is as bad as being <u>condemned to death</u> because his whole world (Juliet) is in Verona. The Friar tries to persuade him that the Prince has been very <u>merciful</u>, but Romeo is beyond listening. Romeo says that cats, dogs, mice and

'every unworthy thing' will be able to 'live in heaven' because they can see Juliet, but he will not. Look carefully at the part of Romeo's speech here where he talks about poison: 'Hast thou no poison mix'd ...'. Romeo is asking the Friar whether he has no other sudden means of death to kill him, as this would be kinder than the word 'banished', which Romeo says is a word which the damned use in hell. The use of <u>potions</u> <u>and</u> <u>poisons</u> is of course an important part of the tragedy and it is connected here with the Friar and later with the apothecary whom Romeo goes to see in Mantua.

The Nurse arrives to tell Romeo of Juliet's dismay at the news. Romeo again <u>blames</u> <u>himself</u> for events. He asks the Friar to tell him in which part of his body his name lives so that he might cut it out.

Art thou a man?

The Friar's long, <u>calm</u> <u>speech</u> here slows down the <u>pace</u> of the action. What he says in this scene is important to the plot and it summarises the basic themes of the play. He says Romeo is

behaving like a wild animal, instead of a man, by letting his emotions get the better of him. He tells Romeo that he has everything to live for and <u>he</u> <u>should</u> <u>count</u> <u>his</u> <u>blessings</u>: Juliet is alive, Tybalt, who wanted to kill him, is dead, and the law – which said he should be executed – has instead said he must only be exiled. Note the Nurse's response to the Friar's speech: 'O Lord, I could have stayed here all the night / To hear good counsel'. How much does she learn from the Friar's words? Compare the 'good counsel' (advice) she gives Juliet in Act 3 Sc 5. Friar Lawrence tells Romeo to go to Juliet and comfort her and then to leave for Mantua before daybreak. The Friar says he will find a way to let everyone know about their marriage, return them to their friends and beg a pardon from the Prince, after which Romeo will be able to return. Romeo is <u>won</u> <u>over</u> by the Friar's <u>reassurance</u> and all seems well until the next scene, when a <u>new</u> <u>twist</u> <u>of</u> <u>fate</u> drives the action towards the tragic conclusion.

Act 3 Scene 4

> **❝*These times of woe afford no times to woo*❞**

Capulet is talking to his guest Paris late on Monday night. He seems to have taken the death of Tybalt with <u>surprising</u> <u>calm</u>. He tells him that Juliet is distraught but that he will speak to her and that he intends the wedding to be <u>brought</u> <u>forward</u> to Thursday. Capulet stresses that it will have to be a quiet occasion out of respect to Tybalt's memory. Capulet gives no reason for this sudden change of mind, nor for the sudden haste. The main hint of a changed situation is Juliet's grief which, ironically, her parents <u>interpret</u> <u>as</u> <u>being</u> <u>for</u> <u>Tybalt's</u> <u>death</u>.

There is <u>extra</u> <u>dramatic</u> <u>tension</u> in this scene because the audience knows that Romeo and Juliet are together in her room upstairs and several times there is raised the possibility that someone may go to speak to her. Out of consideration for her supposed grief, they decide not to disturb her.

This time it is Capulet's actions which bring the tragedy nearer, but again the cause is haste, speed and suddenness. The speed with which events happen in the play is emphasised again. It is now Monday night and the play's action began on Sunday morning, so that a period of only forty-eight hours has been covered. In this time there has been a brawl; Romeo has been in love with Rosaline; Paris has asked to marry Juliet and she has said she will consider it; a banquet has been held; Romeo attended the feast hoping to see Rosaline but has instead seen Juliet; Romeo and Juliet have fallen in love and he has spent the night talking to her in her garden; they have arranged to marry; Friar Laurence has agreed to perform the ceremony and has done so; there has been a second brawl; Tybalt has killed Mercutio; Romeo has killed Tybalt; Romeo has been banished but the Friar has promised to find a way to sort everything out.

Act 3 Scene 5

> **❝** *O God, I have an ill-divining soul* **❞**

Romeo and Juliet have spent their wedding night together in her room. Juliet says that Romeo need not go yet because morning is a long way off. The night is their friend because it allows them to be together. So far in the play, the light of day has been associated with different kinds of hot passion: lust, fighting and anger. Romeo says that as more and more light appears their sadness grows greater and greater.

Juliet claims that the birdsong they can hear is a nightingale and not a lark because she wants him to stay, but Romeo says that morning is here and it is indeed a lark. The animal imagery is used to <u>underline</u> <u>their</u> <u>feelings</u>. Juliet does not want the light in the sky to be that of daybreak because Romeo will have to leave for <u>exile</u> in Mantua. Romeo says that he will agree that it is not day if Juliet wishes, but that this would mean his death if he were to stay and be discovered.

Juliet says she has 'an ill-divining soul' and <u>imagines</u> that she sees Romeo dead <u>in</u> <u>the</u> <u>bottom</u> <u>of</u> <u>a</u> <u>tomb</u>. Both of them are pale, and Romeo says that 'sorrow drinks our blood', meaning that they look pale because they are sad. These are the <u>last</u> <u>words</u> Juliet ever hears from Romeo.

> **❝**he shall soon keep Tybalt company **❞**

Lady Capulet demonstrates her <u>callousness</u> towards Juliet by censuring her supposed grief for Tybalt. She says that showing too much grief is foolish and that it would be better if Juliet were to weep because his murderer Romeo was still alive. The audience knows more than she does, so much of what Juliet says here to her mother will <u>have</u> <u>a</u> <u>different</u> <u>meaning</u> <u>for</u> <u>them</u>. See how many phrases you can find which have a different meaning for Juliet and for Lady Capulet. The audience, knowing the truth, can share in Juliet's <u>deliberate</u> <u>deception</u> of her mother. Notice how <u>calm</u> <u>and</u> <u>mature</u> Juliet is in facing her mother and how much she has changed from the girl we met at the start of the play.

Explore

What do you think about the ways in which Capulet and Lady Capulet respond to Juliet's refusal to marry Paris?

> **❝**Hang thee young baggage, disobedient wretch! **❞**

Capulet arrives and his speech is full of <u>ironic</u> <u>references</u> <u>to</u> <u>storms</u> – ironic because it is he who will storm about in a short while when he hears that Juliet refuses to marry Paris. Notice how <u>cruel</u> Lady Capulet's remark is, and how <u>ominous</u>: 'I would the fool were married to her grave'. This very quickly comes tragically true and is another instance of the <u>image</u> <u>of</u> <u>death</u> as

Juliet's suitor coming to claim her. Capulet flies into a terrible rage at Juliet and tells her she is a <u>traitor</u> and will marry Paris even if he has to <u>drag her to church</u> on a 'hurdle' (a wooden frame used to draw traitors through the streets to their execution). Even Lady Capulet says that her husband is going too far, but he will not be pacified. Capulet says Juliet will never look him in the face again if she disobeys him and says that his 'fingers itch' (to strike her). He tells her she may beg and starve in the streets before he will have her <u>disobey him</u>. Capulet behaves <u>tyrannically</u> and refuses to listen to anyone else.

Even though she is a trusted member of the household, the Nurse is abused by Capulet when she tries to support Juliet. Juliet's parents <u>cannot understand</u> why she does not want to marry a rich husband. This was clearly Lady Capulet's attitude when she married Capulet. Juliet says that unless the marriage can at least be delayed, her bridal bed will be 'in that dim monument where Tybalt lies'. <u>Her mother rejects her</u>: she has 'done with' Juliet. In desperation Juliet <u>turns to her Nurse</u>.

> ❝*I think it best thou married with the County.*❞

The advice that the Nurse gives is that Juliet should <u>make the best of things</u>, keep quiet about her marriage to Romeo and marry Paris. The advice is <u>well-intentioned</u> and the Nurse seems to be trying to <u>comfort</u> and <u>please</u> her mistress, but Juliet is <u>quietly furious</u> and calls her a 'wicked fiend' when she has gone. This marks the severing of Juliet's esteem and friendship for her Nurse. Both Romeo and Juliet are now left almost <u>completely alone</u>, Romeo banished to Mantua and Juliet deserted by those to whom she looked for help and support. Only the Friar <u>remains faithful</u> and even he will <u>fail them</u> at their hour of greatest need in the tomb. Juliet now says that she will try the Friar's plan but, if it fails, she knows she has one final course of action left to her: 'If all else fail, myself have power to die.' Here the coming tragedy is <u>signalled once again</u>.

Quick quiz 3

Uncover the plot

Delete two of the three alternatives given, to find the correct plot.

1   Tybalt, looking to fight Mercutio/Romeo/Benvolio, instead kills Mercutio/Benvolio/Paris when the Prince/Benvolio/Romeo tries to intervene.

2   Tybalt is then killed by an enraged Capulet/Benvolio/Romeo, who is sentenced to death/a fine/banishment.

3   Juliet, distraught, sheds tears over Tybalt's wounds/Romeo's banishment/Tybalt's death. Romeo is told of his fate by Benvolio/the Duke/Friar Lawrence.

4   Juliet is told of the wedding plan by Lady Capulet/Lord Capulet/the Nurse, and refuses. Her father threatens to kill her/poison Romeo/disown her.

5   She is let down even by the Nurse/the Friar/Paris.

Who? What? Where? When? Why? How?

1   What is the 'word there was, worser than Tybalt's death' for Juliet?

2   Why does Lady Capulet think Juliet is weeping?

3   Why does Romeo love Tybalt 'better than thou canst devise'?

4   How does Benvolio say Romeo tried to avoid a fight with Tybalt?

5   How do the lovers tell that dawn is approaching – and how do they try to deny the fact?

Who said that?

1   Who says: 'Mercy but murders, pardoning those that kill'?

2   Who says: 'Either withdraw unto some private place, / Or reason coldly of your grievances'?

3   Who says: 'O calm, dishonourable, vile submission', and why?

4   Who says: 'I would the fool were married to her grave', of whom and why?

Act 4

Act 4 Scene 1

> **❝Love give me strength, and strength shall help afford❞**

Paris explains to Friar Lawrence that Capulet wants the marriage to take place quickly because <u>he</u> <u>is</u> <u>concerned</u> that Juliet is mourning too much for Tybalt's death. There are several <u>ironies</u> here. Juliet is mourning for the banishment of Romeo, for her husband's killing of her cousin and for the death of Tybalt. She has far more cause to grieve than Capulet can possibly know. The suggestion that marriage to Paris will in some way lessen Juliet's grief is obviously another serious error and will instead <u>worsen</u> <u>her</u> <u>situation</u>.

> **❝Venus smiles not in a house of tears❞**

Paris's reference to Venus – the Roman goddess of love – is more appropriate than he knows. As well as the obvious sense, 'house' has an astrological meaning. A 'house' is one of the twelve signs of the zodiac and this again signifies the influence of the stars on the fate of the lovers. This is the only time Paris meets Juliet. Paris is <u>correct</u> and <u>well-mannered</u>, and Juliet is very <u>self-possessed</u> and <u>cool</u> towards him and is clearly not sorry to see him leave.

Juliet says she will <u>do</u> <u>anything</u> to avoid the marriage to Paris. She is <u>desperate</u> and tells the Friar that if he cannot help her she will <u>kill</u> <u>herself</u> with her knife. He says that if she is really determined to be free of Paris so as to be with Romeo, she might find the courage to try his plan. Friar Lawrence tells Juliet that she must <u>secretly</u> <u>take</u> <u>the</u> <u>potion</u> he has made, which will make it look as though she is dead. She will then be put into the Capulets' family tomb. The Friar will send a letter to Romeo and tell him of the plan, so

that he and the Friar can come and rescue Juliet when she wakes up. The Friar's actions in this play, particularly after the banishment of Romeo, are not what you would expect <u>from</u> <u>a</u> <u>holy</u> <u>man</u>, though in his defence it should be said that, but for bad luck, he would have helped Romeo and Juliet to an unexpected happiness. His response is <u>practical</u> rather than <u>moral</u>, despite his lengthy speeches of advice.

Explore

Do you think that the Friar is morally right in helping Romeo and Juliet to their unofficial wedding night and, now, in taking the lead in Juliet's drugging herself to deceive her parents?

The Friar's plan will require <u>great</u> <u>courage</u> of Juliet, especially as she will have to take the potion while she is alone. This <u>increases</u> the <u>audience's</u> <u>sympathy</u> for Juliet. She has become a <u>bold</u> and <u>courageous</u> woman, for she agrees to the Friar's plan without hesitation.

Act 4 Scene 2

> **❝***I'll have this knot knit up tomorrow morning.***❞**

Juliet returns from Friar Lawrence knowing what she must do and she tells her father that she will obey him and marry Paris. Capulet is overjoyed and praises the Friar, saying that the 'whole city is much bound to him'. Capulet <u>assumes</u> that the Friar has persuaded Juliet to obey his wishes and marry Paris. <u>Capulet's</u> <u>praise</u> <u>is</u> <u>ironic</u>, given the Friar's real part in the events that follow. What Juliet could not have anticipated, however, was her father's next move. Capulet decides that the wedding will take place the next day, that is, Wednesday instead of Thursday. This <u>ruins</u> the Friar's plan to write to Romeo. There is no real reason for moving the marriage date in this way. It is as though <u>fate</u> is leaving nothing to chance, just as it seemed once again as though things were about to work out happily for Romeo and Juliet. Juliet feels she has no other option but to go ahead with the Friar's plan and is perhaps not aware of the <u>problems</u> which moving the date has caused the Friar.

Explore

Think about Capulet's plan to bring the wedding forward. Why does he do this? What is its dramatic effect?

Act 4 Scene 3

> **❝**I have a faint cold fear thrills through my veins,
> That almost freezes up the heat of life **❞**

Explore

What does Juliet reveal in her soliloquy? What do you think her state of mind is at this point in the play?

Juliet continues to show great <u>self-control</u> here and, although present, the <u>Nurse</u> <u>says</u> <u>nothing</u>. This is unusual because the Nurse is normally never silent. When the Nurse and Lady Capulet leave, Juliet speaks the <u>soliloquy</u> which takes up the rest of this scene.

The <u>courage</u> and <u>isolation</u> of Juliet are emphasised in this speech. Later on, Romeo will have the same doubts about the poison he buys from the apothecary as those which Juliet has here about the Friar's potion.

Juliet is afraid of what <u>could</u> <u>go</u> <u>wrong</u> with the plan. <u>Ironically</u>, she worries about what might happen if she <u>awakens</u> <u>early</u>, but not about what might go wrong if she <u>awakens</u> <u>too</u> <u>late</u>, which is what actually happens. She has taken the precaution of bringing her knife with her in case the potion does not work at all; she clearly intends to carry out her threatened suicide if this is necessary.

Juliet's <u>haste</u> to take the Friar's potion reveals her <u>desperate</u> <u>state</u> and re-emphasises the <u>speed</u> of <u>dramatic</u> <u>action</u>. All the older characters except the Friar have now rejected Juliet. He too lets her down by failing to get the letter through.

Act 4 Scene 4

> **❝**Go waken Juliet, go and trim her up**❞**

This brief scene concentrates on the minor domestic problems of the Capulets, as they rush around making last-minute

preparations for the wedding. The scene is a <u>sharp contrast</u> to the <u>terror</u> and <u>stillness</u> of the previous scene and also to the next one, when Juliet's body is discovered. Notice how the imagery of the mouth, of food, and of eating and drinking link the scenes together. Capulet makes much mention of <u>time</u> and the need to hurry: the second cock has crowed, the curfew bell has rung, it is three o'clock in the morning. This continual emphasis on speed <u>underlines the feeling of inevitability</u> and of events moving inexorably to their climax.

As dawn breaks for the fourth time in the play and the servants rush about, Capulet again cries for more and more haste and sends the Nurse to rouse Juliet for her wedding.

Explore

Does Lady Capulet also appear less cold at such times?

It might be suggested that Capulet appears in his most favourable light arranging and organising domestic affairs: feasts, parties and so forth. You can no doubt find him bustling and bumbling in a cheerful welcoming haste on more than one occasion in the play.

Act 4 Scene 5

> ❝*She's dead: deceas'd, she's dead, alack the day.*❞

The Nurse is full of chatter about the pleasures of the flesh. She says she hopes Juliet has had plenty of sleep because she will get little rest on her wedding night. This <u>apparent relaxation</u> of the mood actually serves to <u>increase the tension</u> in the play because of the audience's knowledge of what is to happen.

> ❝*Alas, alas! Help, help! My lady's dead!*❞

The Nurse calls for 'aqua vitae' (brandy, although ironically the words literally mean 'water of life'). Lady Capulet cries that unless

Juliet wakes she will die with her. Juliet's father arrives to see his daughter and says that death 'lies on her like an untimely frost'. His words about Juliet <u>reintroduce</u> <u>the</u> <u>flower</u> <u>imagery</u> and are ironic because Juliet's 'untimely' death is <u>not</u> <u>really</u> <u>death</u> <u>at</u> <u>all</u>.

Notice how Shakespeare does not allow the tragedy of this scene to overshadow the <u>**powerful**</u> <u>**impact**</u> of the tragic climax at the end of the play. Shakespeare holds down the tragedy here by keeping this <u>scene</u> <u>short</u> and by placing it between two other sections of <u>lighter</u> <u>mood</u>.

❝ *Death is my son-in-law, death is my heir* **❞**

Capulet tells Paris that death has claimed Juliet for his own, but does so in a way that echoes the sexual death-as-lover imagery in the play. He <u>**connects**</u> it with the imagery of flowers by saying that death has 'deflowered' (taken the virginity of) Juliet.

You will notice that, after the news is broken to Paris, each of the four mourners has a <u>formal</u> <u>speech</u>, all of about the same length, expressing grief. The Friar tells them all to accept heaven's will with good grace. He mentions the image of rosemary – a flower associated with remembrance and the dead – that the Nurse introduced earlier in the play as Juliet's favourite flower, although significantly she linked it then with Romeo.

A <u>comic</u> <u>interlude</u> ends this scene, with the musicians, who have come to play at the wedding, saying to the Nurse that they may as well pack up and be gone. This interlude with Peter may seem rather out of place after what has just happened, but it would be thought too harrowing to move directly from Juliet's 'death' to Romeo's preparation for his.

Uncover the plot

Delete two of the three alternatives given, to find the correct plot.

1   *Paris/the Nurse/Capulet is at Friar Lawrence's cell, informing him that the wedding is now to be on Wednesday/Thursday/Friday.*

2   *Juliet comes to plead for help, saying she will poison herself/jump from a tower/stab herself rather than marry Paris.*

3   *The Friar gives her a 'vial' containing a substance which will make her appear shrunk/dead/asleep for 42/36/24 hours, after which she will awake in the charnel house/graveyard/Capulet vault, to be met by Romeo/Paris/the Nurse.*

4   *Alone, Juliet takes the potion, with a vial of poison/a dagger/a rapier by her side. The family mourn her 'death', restrained by the knowing figure of Capulet/Paris/Friar Lawrence.*

Who? What? Where? When? Why? How?

1   *Who is supposed to find Juliet dead, and who does so?*

2   *What are the symptoms of the Friar's potion?*

3   *What reason does Paris give the Friar for the wedding's being brought forward?*

4   *What does 'the manner of our country' dictate will happen to Juliet when she is found 'dead'?*

5   *Why is Friar Lawrence confident that Juliet will go along with his plan?*

Who said that?

1   *Who says: 'Venus smiles not in a house of tears?*

2   *Who says: 'My dismal scene I needs must act alone'?*

3   *Who says: 'Revive, look up, or I will die with thee!'?*

4   *Who says: 'And weep ye now, seeing she is advanc'd / Above the clouds, as high as heaven itself'?*

Act 5

Act 5 Scene 1

> ❝ *Well Juliet, I will lie with thee tonight* ❞

As his servant arrives in Mantua from Verona, Romeo talks of a prophetic dream he has had where Juliet found him dead. Balthasar has rushed to tell Romeo that he has seen Juliet laid to rest in the Capulet tomb, not knowing the truth. Romeo vows to go to Verona, saying that he will defy the stars, meaning that he defies fate to do any worse to him. It is Romeo's haste at this point that makes the tragedy certain, ignoring Balthasar's counsel to be patient and thus arriving too early for the Friar to intercept him at the tomb.

In his soliloquy, Romeo echoes the imagery of Death lying with Juliet, with its sexual as well as literal meaning – 'Well, Juliet, I will lie with thee tonight' – but the ominous meaning is that he will join her in death.

Romeo goes to an apothecary to buy poison. He says that the apothecary is 'so full of wretchedness' that he should not fear to break the law and risk the death penalty. Look very carefully at Romeo's description of the apothecary and you will see that he is in many ways describing himself: 'the world is not thy friend, nor the world's law'. Romeo's contempt for the gold that he uses to pay for the poison – 'worse poison to men's souls' – is an ironic comment on the attitude of Juliet's parents to true love; 'the great rich Capulet' and his callous wife who think, like the Nurse, that marriage is merely to do with physical passion or a commercial transaction. 'I sell thee poison, thou hast sold me none' he says to the apothecary, and gives him forty gold coins (ducats). This scene is another important turning-point in

Explore

Think about the character of the apothecary. Why do you think Shakespeare included him? Does he add anything to the play?

the action of the play and you will see many <u>similarities</u> between it and the marriage scene in the Friar's cell; notice the <u>parallels of</u> <u>tone</u> and <u>imagery</u>.

Act 5 Scene 2

> 66 *Now I must to the monument alone.* 99

<u>Bad</u> <u>luck</u> <u>strikes</u> <u>again</u> as Friar John tells Friar Lawrence that he was delayed getting out of the city to deliver the message to Romeo because an outbreak of plague prevented him leaving an infected house. He returns the Friar's letter to Romeo undelivered.

Explore

What dramatic effect does the news that Romeo has not received Friar Lawrence's letter have?

The action again <u>speeds</u> <u>up</u> after the last quiet scene as Friar Lawrence is <u>thrown</u> <u>into</u> <u>despair</u> by this news. Juliet is due to awaken within three hours. Friar Lawrence will go and get her from the tomb and hide her in his cell until another message can be sent to Romeo. Friar Lawrence has always had a <u>calm</u> <u>solution</u> to each situation. The <u>build-up</u> <u>of</u> <u>tension</u> is therefore increased when we find him <u>in</u> <u>haste</u>, talking of <u>danger</u> and sending for a crowbar. Once again, though, the ingenious Friar has a solution, explained in his <u>brief</u> <u>soliloquy</u>. This time the audience knows that his solution will not work: why?

Act 5 Scene 3

> 66 *Sweet flower, with flowers thy bridal bed I strew* 99

Paris has come at night to Juliet's tomb to visit his 'sweet flower', put flowers on her grave and pay his respects. Although he seems <u>rather</u> <u>formal</u> and <u>sentimental</u> <u>in</u> <u>his</u> <u>speech</u>, he is <u>genuinely</u> <u>sincere</u> in the same way that Romeo was sincere in his love-sickness for Rosaline. His comment on

Text commentary

hearing his servant's warning whistle is <u>ironic</u>: 'what cursed foot wanders this way tonight', because we know it is Romeo. This whole scene is filled with <u>ironic</u> <u>parallels</u>. Paris <u>anticipates</u> events by thinking that Juliet has died of grief for Tybalt, when she is soon to die of grief for Romeo. Just as Romeo hid in the darkness and overheard Juliet first speak of her love for him, so here Paris hides in the darkness and overhears Romeo at her tomb. Paris, the rival lover, brings flowers to the tomb of Juliet and meets the other 'rival lover' in the play, death, in the form of Romeo.

Paris thinks that Romeo has come to pursue the family feud by revenging himself on Juliet's dead body and he asks one of the play's central questions when he says 'can vengeance be pursu'd further than death?' Paris interrupts Romeo and with <u>unconscious</u> <u>irony</u> tells him 'thou must die'.

Romeo's sad reply is an <u>echo</u> <u>of</u> <u>his</u> <u>reply</u> to Tybalt's invitation to fight with him: he tells Paris 'I love thee better than myself'. Paris's servant sees them fighting and runs for help, but Paris is killed. This fatal confrontation marks the only time in the play when Paris and Romeo actually meet.

> **❝❝**_her beauty makes This vault a feasting presence full of light._**❞❞**

Romeo says he will bury Paris with Juliet but that it will not be in a grave but in 'a lantern', because Juliet's beauty makes the tomb 'full of light'. Again the beauty of Juliet is <u>compared</u> by Romeo to <u>brilliant</u> <u>light</u>, even in death, and his speech is full of word-play on '<u>lightning</u>', which should remind you of Juliet's worry that their love resembled lightning too much. The lovers' passion has been described by the <u>imagery</u> as <u>almost</u> <u>religious</u> and <u>heavenly</u>, and the Friar warned that too much <u>passion</u> was dangerous and would <u>consume</u> <u>itself</u> 'like fire and powder'.

Explore

What do you notice about the imagery Romeo uses when he sees Juliet? What effect does this imagery create?

Romeo's long and final speech in the play is a beautiful soliloquy in which death is spoken of as sucking 'the honey' of Juliet's

breath. Ironically Romeo, thinking that Juliet is <u>beautiful</u> <u>even</u> <u>in</u> <u>death</u>, remarks that it has 'no power' over her beauty and her lips and cheeks are still crimson. He does not know that the colour is returning to her lips and cheeks because she is about to awaken and thinks instead that 'Death is amorous' and keeps her ever-beautiful in the tomb to be his lover. The play's <u>images</u> of the <u>dawn</u> and <u>fire</u> and <u>light</u> <u>symbolising</u> the beauty that chases away the darkness of night have finally met in this last <u>mysterious</u> <u>irony</u>; here at the final dawn in the play, Juliet is Life in Death. Romeo drinks the poison and dies, and within a few lines Juliet is awake and asking for him by name. Romeo has been <u>destroyed</u> <u>by</u> <u>fate</u> and his <u>impetuous</u> <u>haste</u> has been his <u>final</u> <u>undoing</u>. The imagery of drinking has come full circle from its start in the joy of life at Capulet's feast to this point of death and tragedy.

> **❝** *This is thy sheath; there rest, and let me die.* **❞**

The Friar arrives but is too late to save the lives of Paris or Romeo. He urges the awakened Juliet to escape with him and <u>underlines</u> <u>the</u> <u>role</u> <u>of</u> <u>fate</u> in the play when he tells her that 'a greater power than we can contradict hath thwarted our intents'. Unable to persuade her to leave, the Friar <u>panics</u> <u>and</u> <u>runs</u> <u>away</u>.

The last <u>reference</u> to <u>drinking</u> in the play occurs when Juliet cannot find a 'friendly drop' of poison in the cup in Romeo's hand. She kills herself with the dagger in order to be with her husband in death. Juliet's suicide is the traditional death of the noble warrior who is defeated but will not be enslaved. This is a fitting end for someone who has been throughout the <u>stronger</u> and more <u>practical</u> <u>of</u> <u>the</u> <u>lovers</u> and who has had to face <u>danger</u> <u>alone</u>.

Explore

Do you feel that, at the end of the play, the Capulets and Montagues have been equally punished by fate for their feud?

Servants and watchmen appear, discover the bodies of Paris, Romeo and Juliet, and arrest Romeo's servant Balthasar and Friar

Lawrence pending Prince Escalus's arrival. Lord and Lady Capulet enter, followed by the Prince. Montague arrives with the news that his wife has died of grief over Romeo's exile.

> **❝ *O brother Montague, give me thy hand.* ❞**

Friar Lawrence makes a long chorus-like speech near the end of the play in which he reviews what has happened. This dramatic device enables Shakespeare to ensure that the audience understands and remembers the plot of the play and, by allowing Balthasar to complete the story, introduces the letter from Romeo to support the Friar's account and to reveal the events in Mantua.

Appropriately, it is the fiery-tempered Capulet who asks for Montague's hand in peace. The feuding families agree to live in peace and say they will put up golden statues to Romeo and Juliet. The appearance of the Prince at the very end of the play emphasises the political point of the play: that society depends upon order and obedience to authority. The Prince proclaims these things on each of his three appearances. The imagery of light is used finally by the Prince when he says that on this last day 'the sun for sorrow will not show his head', finally underlining the darkness (in many senses) in which the play closes and the way heaven is in sympathy with the dead lovers.

Of all the six characters who die in the play, only the loving Lady Montague is not young. This underlines how the play concentrates on the passionate world of the young and the way in which it is they who must pay the price for the mischievous and quarrelsome folly of the old.

Uncover the plot

Delete two of the three alternatives given, to find the correct plot.

1   *Benvolio/Friar John/Balthasar arrives in Verona/Mantua/Venice with news of Juliet's early marriage/escape plan/death.*

2   *Romeo seeks out a Franciscan Friar/beggar/apothecary to buy a cordial/poison/dagger. Meanwhile, Friar Lawrence learns that his messenger Friar John/Balthasar/Friar Francis has not got through.*

3   *Capulet/Paris/Montague is at the vault when Romeo arrives, tries to arrest/kill/fight him, and is killed. Wondering that Juliet looks so pale/merry/fair, Romeo poisons himself.*

4   *Friar Lawrence/Balthasar/the Page arrives too late. Juliet, finding Romeo dead, kills herself with the dregs of the poison/the poison on his lips/his dagger.*

Who? What? Where? When? Why? How?

1   *Who is asked to account for events, following the discovery of the bodies in the vault?*

2   *Who is the first to ask for his former enemy's hand in peace?*

3   *What has happened to Lady Montague?*

4   *What is Friar Lawrence's emergency plan, when he realises the first has failed?*

5   *Where was Friar John delayed, and why?*

6   *Why does Friar Lawrence flee?*

Who said that?

1   *Who says: 'If I may trust the flattering truth of sleep / My dreams presage some joyful news at hand' – and why is this ironic?*

2   *Who says: 'Thou detestable maw, thou womb of death / Gorg'd with the dearest morsel of the earth'?*

3   *Who says: 'Can vengeance be pursued further than death?' – and why, and what more does this say to the audience of the play?*

4   *Who says: 'And I, for winking at your discords too, / Have lost a brace of kinsmen'?*

Writing essays on *Romeo and Juliet*

Exams

- To prepare for an exam, you should read the text through *at least twice*, preferably *three times*. In order to answer an exam question on it you need to know it very well.

- When studying a play, such as *Romeo and Juliet*, you should try to see a performance of it. If you cannot see a live performance on stage, you should watch it on video or DVD. There are several versions available and you should be able to get a copy through your local library.

- If you are studying the text for an 'open book' exam, make sure that you take your copy of the text with you. However, do not rely on it too much – you haven't got time. If you are not allowed to take the text in with you, you will need to memorise brief quotations.

- Read all the questions carefully before deciding which one you are going to answer. Choose the question that best allows you to demonstrate your understanding and personal ideas.

- Make sure that you understand exactly what the question is asking you to do.

- Plan your answer carefully before starting to write your essay (see page 70).

- Always begin your answer with a short introduction which gives an overview of the topic. Use your plan to help keep you focused on the question as you write the essay. Try to leave enough time to write a brief conclusion.

- Remember to use the **point–quotation–comment** approach, where you make a point, support it with a short quotation, then comment on it. Use short and relevant quotations – do not waste time copying out chunks of the text.

- Make sure that you know how much time you have for each question and stick to it.

- Leave enough time at the end of the exam to check your work through carefully and correct any spelling or other mistakes that you have made.

- Timing is not as crucial for coursework essays, so this is your chance to show what you can really do, without having to write under pressure. Do not leave your coursework essays until the last minute though. If you have to rush your work it is unlikely to be the best you can produce.

- Coursework allows you to go into more detail and develop your ideas in greater depth. The required length of assignments varies, and your teacher will advise you on this.

- If you have a choice of title, make sure you choose one which you are interested in and which gives you the chance to develop your ideas.

- Plan your essay carefully (see page 70). Refer to your plan and the essay title as you write, to check that you are staying on course.

- Use quotations in your essay, but beware of using them **too frequently** or making them **too long**. Often, the best quotes are just one or two words or short phrases. Make sure that they are relevant to the points that you are making.

- If your topic requires it, use appropriate background information and put the text in a cultural and historical context. Remember, though, that the text itself should be at the centre of your essay.

- Include a short conclusion which sums up the key points of your ideas.

- Do not copy any of your essay from another source, e.g. other notes or the Internet. This is called plagiarism, and it is very serious if the exam board find that you have done this.

- If you have used sources, list them in a bibliography at the end of the essay.

- If you are allowed to word process your essay, it will be easier to make changes and to re-draft it.

Writing essays

> *Some consequence yet hanging in the stars,*
> *Shall bitterly begin his fearful date,*
> *With this night's revels*   *(Act 1 Sc 4)*

These lines are spoken by Romeo as he and his friends are on their way to the Capulet ball. They can be used to show how Romeo feels misgivings about what is going to happen. It can also show how he feels that he is in the hands of fate.

> *O she doth teach the torches to burn bright:*
> *It seems she hangs upon the cheek of night,*
> *As a rich jewel in an Ethiop's ear* *(Act 1 Sc 5)*

These lines are spoken by Romeo when he first sees Juliet at the Capulet ball. They can be used to show the impact she has on him and how it is a case of 'love at first sight'. It also shows the richness of the language and imagery that Romeo uses to express his feelings.

> *O Romeo, Romeo, wherefore art thou Romeo?*
> *Deny thy father and refuse thy name.* *(Act 2 Sc2)*

These lines are spoken by Juliet at the beginning of the 'balcony scene' when she is thinking alone. They can be used to show how she is aware of the possible problem caused by Romeo being a Montague.

> *These violent delights have violent ends,*
> *And in their triumph die like fire and powder:*
> *Which as they kiss consume.* *(Act 2 Sc 6)*

These lines are spoken by Friar Lawrence when he speaks to

Romeo. He is trying to persuade Romeo to be patient in his love for Juliet. The quotation can be used to show how the Friar is aware of the dangers of violent passions. It also is prophetic in that in the end Romeo's and Juliet's love destroys them both.

> **"** *a plague a' both your houses,*
> *They have made worms' meat of me,*
> *I have it, and soundly, to your houses.* **"** *(Act 3 Sc 1)*

These lines are spoken by Mercutio after being fatally wounded by Tybalt. They can be used to show the destructive consequences of the feud.

> **"** *O my love, my wife,*
> *Death that hath sucked the honey of thy breath,*
> *Hath had no power yet upon thy beauty* **"** *(Act 5 Sc 3)*

These lines are spoken by Romeo when he finds Juliet's body in the vault and believes that she is dead. They can be used to show Romeo's love for Juliet and his admiration of her beauty. They can also be used to illustrate how Shakespeare uses imagery associated with death.

> **"** *Capulet, Montague?*
> *See what a scourge is laid upon your hate!*
> *That heaven finds means to kill your joys with love* **"**
> *(Act 5 Sc 3)*

These lines are spoken by the Prince at the end of the play. They can be used to show how the feud has destroyed the children of Capulet and Montague, and the pointless waste of young lives it has caused.

1. *Explore the presentation of Tybalt, and his contribution to the overall effect of* Romeo and Juliet.

2. *Compare the characters of Romeo and Juliet in the play. You should use details from the text to support your ideas.*

3. *Discuss the view that the tragedy which befalls Romeo and Juliet comes about as a result of simple 'bad luck'.*

4. *The action of the play begins on Sunday morning, and by Thursday morning, Mercutio, Tybalt, Romeo, Juliet and Paris are all dead. Why does Shakespeare create his plot around such a short time scheme?*

5. *Examine Shakespeare's use of poetry and prose in* Romeo and Juliet.

6. *Discuss the character of Mercutio and his contribution to the overall effect of the play.*

7. *How does Romeo change during the course of the play?*

8. *Choose* **two** *scenes or incidents from the play which you find dramatically effective. Discuss the ways in which Shakespeare gives these parts of the play a particular impact.*

9. *How does Shakepseare use imagery associated with death in the play, and what effects does this create?*

10. *What does Shakespeare have to say about the nature of love and hate in the play?*

11. *Examine the role played by fate and coincidence in* Romeo and Juliet.

12. *Discuss the role of Friar Lawrence in* Romeo and Juliet.

13. *How do the comic elements of* Romeo and Juliet *contribute to the overall effect of the play?*

14. *Examine the ways in which Shakespeare uses dramatic irony in* Romeo and Juliet. *What effect does this have on the play?*

15. *Compare and contrast the Capulet and Montague families.*

16. Romeo and Juliet *is a play rich in imagery. Examine the ways in which Shakespeare uses imagery, and the contribution it makes to the overall effect of the play.*

17. *How does Romeo change during the course of the play?*

18. *What do you learn from* Romeo and Juliet *about Elizabethan attitudes to love and marriage?*

19. *Discuss Shakespeare's use of soliloquies in* Romeo and Juliet *and how they contribute to the dramatic effect of the play.*

20. *Examine the role of a) the Nurse and b) Benvolio in* Romeo and Juliet.

In order to write an effective essay, you need to approach your task in an organised way. You need to plan your essay carefully before beginning to write. This will help you to achieve a higher grade.

- The first thing to do is read the question carefully to make sure that you fully understand it, then highlight key words.

- You will need to make notes on the topic in order to start preparing your ideas. You can do this in various ways, such as making a list of key points, or creating a spidergram or a mind map.

- One advantage of using mind maps or spidergrams is that they help you to create links between the various points you make. Put the title of the essay in the middle of a page and add your points around it. You can then draw lines to connect up various points or ideas, linking them in a clear, visual way.

- If you wish, you can colour code your ideas, or even add pictures or symbols if that helps you to think about your ideas more clearly.

- Since mind maps and spidergrams are a way of charting your knowledge, they are also an excellent revision aid. You could work through a number of essay titles in this way. (See some examples of spidergrams on the following pages.)

- In the planning stage of your essay it is also a good idea to jot down some useful quotations. These should be kept brief and to the point, and can be added to your spidergram.

- It can also be useful to plan what you are going to write in each paragraph of your essay. You can number the branches on your spidergram, so that you are clear about the order of your points. This will help you to structure your work more effectively.

- Remember that you are much more likely to write an effective essay if you do some planning before you start to write it.

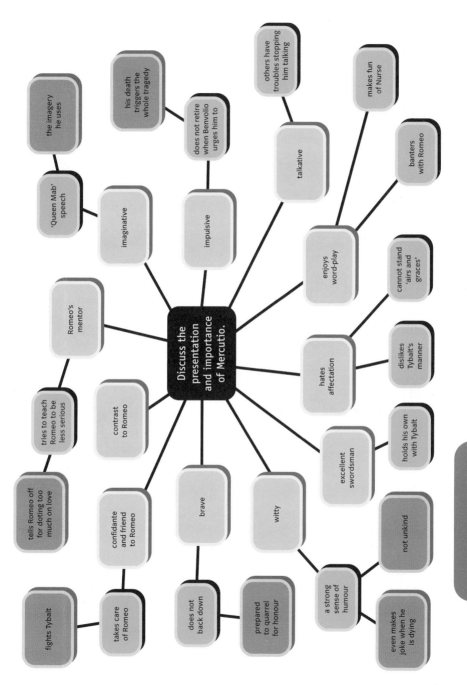

Discuss the presentation and importance of Mercutio.

- the imagery he uses
  - 'Queen Mab' speech
- his death triggers the whole tragedy
- does not retire when Benvolio urges him to
- imaginative
- impulsive
- others have troubles stopping him talking
- makes fun of Nurse
- talkative
- banters with Romeo
- enjoys word-play
- Romeo's mentor
  - tries to teach Romeo to be less serious
  - tells Romeo off for doting too much on love
- cannot stand 'airs and graces'
- dislikes Tybalt's manner
- hates affectation
- contrast to Romeo
- confidante and friend to Romeo
  - takes care of Romeo
    - fights Tybalt
- brave
  - does not back down
  - prepared to quarrel for honour
- excellent swordsman
  - holds his own with Tybalt
- witty
  - a strong sense of humour
    - even makes joke when he is dying
- not unkind

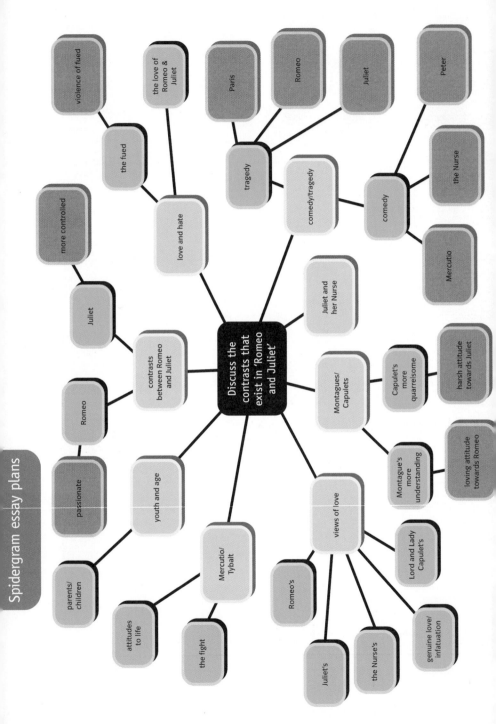

The diagram maps ideas for the essay question "Discuss the contrasts that exist in 'Romeo and Juliet'".

- **love and hate**
  - the fued
    - violence of fued
  - the love of Romeo & Juliet
- **comedy/tragedy**
  - tragedy
    - Paris
    - Romeo
    - Juliet
    - Peter
  - comedy
    - the Nurse
    - Mercutio
- **Juliet and her Nurse**
- **contrasts between Romeo and Juliet**
  - Juliet
    - more controlled
  - Romeo
    - passionate
- **youth and age**
  - parents/children
- **Mercutio/Tybalt**
  - attitudes to life
  - the fight
- **views of love**
  - Romeo's
  - Juliet's
  - the Nurse's
  - genuine love/infatuation
  - Lord and Lady Capulet's
- **Montagues/Capulets**
  - Capulet's more quarrelsome
    - harsh attitude towards Juliet
  - Montague's more understanding
    - loving attitude towards Romeo

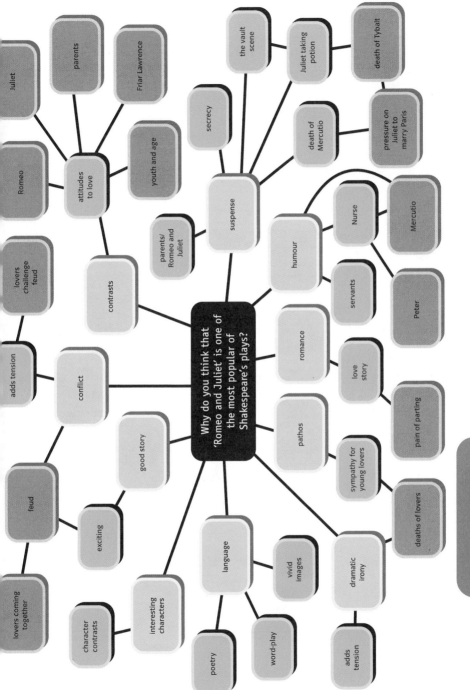

Why do you think that 'Romeo and Juliet' is one of the most popular of Shakespeare's plays?

- attitudes to love
  - Juliet
  - parents
  - Friar Lawrence
  - Romeo
  - youth and age
- contrasts
  - lovers challenge feud
  - parents/ Romeo and Juliet
- suspense
  - the vault scene
  - Juliet taking potion
  - death of Tybalt
  - secrecy
  - death of Mercutio
  - pressure on Juliet to marry Paris
- humour
  - Nurse
  - Mercutio
  - servants
  - Peter
- conflict
  - adds tension
  - feud
  - lovers coming together
- good story
  - exciting
- romance
  - love story
- pathos
  - sympathy for young lovers
  - pain of parting
  - deaths of lovers
- interesting characters
  - character contrasts
- language
  - vivid images
  - poetry
  - word-play
- dramatic irony
  - adds tension

Sample response

(a) Discuss the character of Friar Lawrence and his role in the play.

(b) Imagine that Friar Lawrence writes a letter to Prince Escalus, explaining what he has done and why. Write the letter, including all the things that you think he might have said.

(a) Friar Lawrence proves he is not a brave man by showing his fear ✓ all the way through the play. He says things like, 'fear comes upon me, O, much I fear some ill unthrifty thing' and, 'I dare no longer stay' ✓ and, 'I'll dispose of thee among a sisterhood of holy nuns', in other words he's trying to cover up what he's done.✓ He did try to say 'no' to marrying Romeo and Juliet by suggesting that Romeo moves easily from one love to the next. ✓ He says, 'To lay one in, another out to have' and, 'Affliction is enamoured of thy parts, And thou art wedded to calamity', meaning bad luck ✓ seems to follow Romeo everywhere. Friar Lawrence tells Romeo that he loves like one who recites from a book without the ability to understand what he memorises ✓ by saying, 'Thy love did read by rote, that could not spell'.

Friar Lawrence hopes the wedding of Romeo and Juliet will help the Montague's and Capulet's be friends again. ✓ He says, 'so smile the heavens upon this holy act that after-hours with sorrow chide us not', meaning let heaven smile on us all so that this wedding will not be regretted by anyone.

(b) Dear Prince Escalus

I am writing to you, not only to ask for your forgiveness but to ask for your understanding. When Romeo came to me to ask me to marry Juliet and himself I was very shocked. He begged and pleaded with me, so in the end I decided to go ahead and marry them the next day. ✓

Romeo and I waited patiently for Juliet to arrive, and when she did I had to pry them apart in order to marry them. I could see straight away that they were lusting after each other. Later that day Mercutio was killed by Tybalt, so Romeo killed Tybalt. Of course, Juliet was upset by the news of Tybalt's death but was more upset by Romeo's banishment to Mantua. ✓ She was also upset and frightened about her marriage to Paris.

Juliet came to me looking for a way out. I gave her a potion which would put her to sleep for a few hours. She was to wake up after she was laid in the tomb, but because the letter that I sent to Romeo didn't get there, he thought she was really dead and therefore killed himself. When I got there, Juliet was just waking up and she saw Romeo's lifeless body on the floor. I was frightened so I ran away and left Juliet there, which is when she took her own life. ✓

I am deeply sorry for the upset I have caused, but I honestly thought I was doing the right thing. ✓ My hopes were that the two families would become friends. Again I would like to say how sorry I am about everything and I beg you for your forgiveness

Your Humble Servant

Friar Lawrence

Examiner's comments

(a) This is a sound response in which the candidate shows a clear understanding of some key aspects of Friar Lawrence, although the view of the character is rather narrow. Some insight and evaluation is evident and textual references used. However, the quotations could be used to develop the discussion further, and overall the response is rather brief and under-developed.

(b) The letter captures an appropriate tone and style effectively, and also shows a clear understanding of the Friar's standpoint and what went wrong. Again, the response could be developed further, and the Friar's motives for doing what he did and his feelings at the tragic outcome explored in a little more depth.

Sample response

(a) Discuss the character of Friar Lawrence and his role in the play.

(b) Imagine that Friar Lawrence writes a letter to Prince Escalus explaining what he has done and why. Write the letter including all the things that you think he might have said.

(a) We first encounter Friar Lawrence at dawn, gathering herbs. ✓ The Friar is instantly aware that Romeo must be troubled ✓ if he seeks him at such an early hour. When Romeo requests that the Friar marry him to Juliet, he is quick to point out Romeo's infatuation ✓ for Rosaline and questions his love for Juliet, forcing Romeo to assess his own situation.✓ He chides Romeo 'For doting not for loving pupil mine'. The Friar is a compassionate ✓ and worldly man. He believes that the marriage of Romeo and Juliet could resolve the bitter feuding of the Capulets and Montagues, ✓ so he agrees to marry them that afternoon.

Friar Lawrence demonstrates that he is a moral and holy man. ✓ He wants to ensure that Romeo and Juliet's love is sanctified in the sight of God before their love is consummated, 'For by your leaves, you shall not stay alone, Till Holy Church incorporate two in one.' ✓

The Friar takes on the role of counsellor to Romeo, ✓ who is devastated when the Friar informs him he is to be banished to Mantua for slaying Tybalt.

In Act 4, Scene 1 Juliet shows complete trust by confiding to the Friar her despair at having to marry Paris and asks him for a means to prevent the forthcoming marriage. He gives her a vial of potion he has concocted ✓ to take while in bed that evening, which will make her appear dead for 42 hours. He tells Juliet of his plan to send for Romeo to come to Juliet at the Capulet tomb. Again, he inspires hope in Juliet ✓.

The Friar panics when he realises that Romeo has not received his letter, but tries to rectify the matter by sending another urgent message, hoping Romeo will receive it in time.

(b) Dear Prince Escalus

It is with great sadness that I write this letter. I must confess that I am responsible for marrying Romeo and Juliet. The reason I was compelled to do this was not only because of their great love for each other, but as a means of ending the bitter feud between the Capulet and Montague families. ✓ Alas, events have taken a tragic course. After the marriage, Romeo slew Tybalt and was banished to Manuta. He was inconsolable at being separated from his beloved Juliet. Juliet came to me to ask me to devise some means to stop this second marriage, otherwise she would kill herself. You can imagine the dilemma I was in. What should I do? ✓

I decided to give Juliet a potion which would make her appear dead for 42 hours. She took it that night and was found, as though dead, the following morning by her Nurse.

I bear the guilt of this tragedy on my shoulders and pray you will understand. I truly believed I was working for the good of both families. ✓ My dearest wish is that you will not consider me a bad man because of this, but will see my good intentions.

Yours truly

Friar Lawrence.

Examiner's comments

(a) A perceptive, detailed and thorough response which balances various aspects of the Friar's character. A wide range of relevant points are made, with some well-chosen textual support. The structure of the essay is good, and points are developed and connections made in an effective way. Overall an excellent understanding of the character of Friar Lawrence is shown.

(b) An excellent letter that convincingly captures the voice of the character and shows first-class knowledge of the text. A range of points are made, based on a perceptive reading of the text.

Quick quiz answers

Quick quiz 1
Uncover the plot
1 Verona; the Prince
2 Benvolio; Rosaline
3 Paris
4 Lady Capulet
5 Capulet
6 my only hate

Who? What? When? Where? Why? How?
1 Queen Mab 1,4
2 Juliet 1, 5
3 a crutch 1,1
4 Sampson 'biting his thumb' at Abraham and Balthasar 1,1
5 in a sycamore grove west of the city 1,1
6 because Romeo behaves well, is well spoken of in Verona, and is under Capulet's roof 1,5
7 by his voice; because he is wearing a mask 1,5
8 three 1,1

Who said that?
1 Benvolio 1,1
2 Romeo 1,1
3 Mercutio 1,4
4 Capulet – repeating the general opinion of Verona 1,5
5 Tybalt 1,1

Quick quiz 2
Uncover the plot
1 Romeo
2 'I'll take thee at thy word'
3 her kinsmen will kill him
4 Tybalt
5 blushes
6 the Friar's cell

Who? What? When? Where? Why? How?
1 Tybalt 2,4
2 Mercutio 2,4
3 (a) Romeo will 'deny (his) father and refuse (his) name' or (b) she will 'no longer be a Capulet' 2,2
4 'Stony limits' (Juliet's wall) 2,2
5 Why – not 'where'! She is saying: why did you have to be Romeo – a Montague? 2,2
6 To church, for confession and absolution ('shrift') 2,5
7 In the orchard below Juliet's room 2,2
8 For 'doting' on – not for 'loving' – Rosaline 2,3

Who said that?
1 Juliet 2,2
2 Friar Lawrence 2,3
3 Mercutio 2,4
4 Romeo 2,6
5 Nurse 2,5

Quick quiz 3
Uncover the plot
1 Romeo; Mercutio; Romeo
2 Romeo; banishment
3 Romeo's banishment; Friar Lawrence
4 Lady Capulet; disown her
5 the Nurse

Who? What? Where? When? Why? How?
1 'banished' 3,2
2 because Tybalt is dead and Romeo lives 3,5
3 because – unknown to Tybalt – they are now related by marriage 3,1

4 by 'speaking fair', and by pleading the triviality of the quarrel and the Prince's displeasure 3,1

5 the lark (said to be a nightingale), and first light (said to be a meteor or moonglow) 3,5

Who said that?

1 the Prince 3,1

2 Benvolio 3,1

3 Mercutio, because Romeo is refusing to fight Tybalt 3,1

4 Lady Capulet of juliet, because she refuses to be married to Paris 3,5

Quick quiz 4

Uncover the plot

1 Paris; Thursday

2 stab herself

3 dead; 42 hours; Capulet vault; Romeo

4 dagger; Friar Lawrence

Who? What? Where? When? Why? How?

1 the bridegroom (Paris) 4,1; the Nurse 4,4

2 cold, stiffness, stopping of breath and pulse, pallor, closed eyes 4,1

3 Capulet thinks Juliet's grief for Tybalt is harmful 4,1

4 she will be dressed in her best robes and carried on an open bier to the Capulet vault 4,1

5 because she has 'the strength of will' to kill herself rather than marry Paris 4,1

Who said that?

1 Paris 4,1

2 Juliet 4,3

3 Lady Capulet 4,5

4 Friar Lawrence 4,5

Quick quiz 5

Uncover the plot

1 Balthasar; Mantua; death

2 apothecary; poison; Friar John

3 Paris; fight him; fair

4 Friar Lawrence; his dagger

Who? What? Where? When? Why? How?

1 Balthasar, Friar Lawrence and Paris, page 5,3

2 Capulet 5,3

3 she has died of grief at Romeo's banishment 5,3

4 to write again to Mantua, meanwhile hiding Juliet in his cell 5,2

5 in Verona, because his companion friar had been visiting the sick and both were quarantined for being infectious 5,2

6 because he hears the watch coming 5,3

Who said that?

1 Romeo, because he can't trust the dream: there is only bad news ahead 5,1

2 Romeo 5,3

3 Paris, because he thinks Romeo is avenging himself on Juliet's body; in fact, love conquers vengeance only through the death of the lovers 5,3

4 the Prince 5,3

Page 14, Shakespeare, © Robert Harding World Imagery / Robert Harding Picture Library / Alamy.com
Page 16, Scene, © Twentieth Century Fox / Everett / Rex Features

First published 1994
Revised edition 2004

Letts Educational
Chiswick Centre
414 Chiswick High Road
London W4 5TF
Tel: 020 8996 3333

Cover and text design by Hardlines Ltd., Charlbury, Oxfordshire.

Typeset by Letterpart Ltd., Reigate, Surrey.

Graphic illustration by Beehive Illustration, Cirencester, Gloucestershire.

Commissioned by Cassandra Birmingham

Editorial project management by Jo Kemp

Printed in Italy.

British Library Cataloguing in Publication Data. A CIP record of this book is available from the British Library.

ISBN 1 84315 316·5

Letts Educational is a division of Granada Learning, part of Granada plc.